Personal Accountability and Power

How Contractors Can Build a Stronger Safety Culture

by **Tom Esch**
President of Esch Consulting, LLC

www.EschConsulting.com

Personal Accountability and POWER:
How Contractors Can Build a Stronger Safety Culture
by Tom Esch

For information, contact
BDI Publishers, Atlanta, Georgia,
bdipublishers@gmail.com.

Cover Design and Layout: Tudor Maier

BDI Publishers

Atlanta, Georgia

ISBN: 978-1-946637-21-5
FIRST EDITION

Tom is one of the more skilled leadership and organizational development consultants I've worked with in my decades of leadership, including 16 years in the commercial nuclear power industry. We needed more focus on the development of our first line leaders to effect real change in our culture than what we were able to provide due to other demands. Tom was able to efficiently and effectively fill that need. We have seen a step change in how our first line leaders interact with our individual contributors that has been proven in measurable industrial safety improvements and fewer conflicts that are managed at the correct level within the organization. I commend Tom and this excellent, quick read to you.

Steve Andersen, P.E., Division Manager, City of Omaha
Sewer Maintenance and Flood Control

How many people can train others on the people side of safety? Tom's book is about how we interact and communicate at the most basic, yet subtle, levels. Sit back and enjoy this easy read.

Carl Vasquez, CSP, NUCA Director of Education,
Training and Safety

Tom's passion for safety is reflected in his commitment to not only educate about safe work practices, but to change the safety culture of companies, encompassing all executives and employees.

Mike Wiedmaier, Executive Director of the
Utility Contractor Association (UCA), Chicago, Illinois

Tom is an engaging facilitator that takes a hands-on approach helping others understand the benefits of the often neglected personal and behavioral side of safety. His focus and passion for communication and building mutually beneficial relationships helps anyone willing to put in the effort to improve. He leads by example and adds value to all that he interacts with.

Adam Tripp CSP, Safety Services Manager
TBG – The Builders Group, Minnesota

Tom hits the nail on the head with how we can relate to our coworkers in a more meaningful way. Showing them that they are needed and appreciated creates a team which operates safely, creates synergy, and brings profits to your organization.

Joe Holtmeier, Holtmeier Construction

Tom has trained and worked with the best of the best, but he's also seen the rest. His valuable experience has set him apart to provide this great book to help those that need to hear it most.

Perry Silvey, CHST, BT Construction, Inc.

Tom's writing is insightfully convincing and thought provoking. His arguments show how errors in teamwork and communication lead to catastrophe throughout a spectrum of differing environments from the highly technical to that of the non-skilled. Tom provides an effective and powerful framework for leading in ranked societies. His examples of cultures of power which pervade our society demonstrates how directional leadership changes can be made in order to make one's group accountable and focused. This framework has enabled me to look at how accountability is a factor of the power that we possess and how to encourage everyone within a leader's sphere to operate without loss of respect or control. This book is a must read for all leaders.

Brian E. Delahaut, Vice President, MK Diamond, Inc

Tom's knowledge of the construction industry, his Catholic faith, and his humor offers an inspirational perspective on communication and safety. Excellent read!

Mike & Patty Stark, Stark & Son Trenching, Inc.,
Burlington, Illinois

Tom has a unique insight for construction site safety that resonates throughout this book. His understanding of the construction culture, the hierarchy of "rank" and tenure, and the interplay between them allows him to demonstrate the impact of philosophy and application of Safety and safe work practices for construction companies and the construction industry.

Rick Norland P.E, Owner, Construction Solutions, LLC

Tom is an inspirational speaker/writer/mentor. His ability to draw you in and explain how he sees the world is likely to have a positive impact on your world. People is what Tom is all about. People communicating skillfully and going home to their families, safely, every day. Great book Tom, glad you're in the construction "missionary business" now.

Dave Ruddy, CHST, Blue Sky Safety Consulting, LLC,
Denver, Colorado

Tom Esch uses his vast knowledge of the industry and the people in it, along with his background as a priest, to create an amazing book that speaks directly to both managers and workers. With grace and compassion, he tells heartfelt stories, and offers practical methods that will help any company improve their safety practices. The content of this book, taken seriously, can lower your risks of injury and death. Dig in and start applying Tom's wisdom to your current safety program today!

Brent Darnell, Owner of BDI Publishing

This book is a very practical book that is easy to understand and implement practices that will ultimately help your business' success. I highly recommend reading this book.

Chad Burdick, Constructors, Lincoln, Nebraska

Tom's one-of-a-kind life experiences give him a unique perspective. Tom teaches companies and workers to safely navigate the intersection of the fragility of life and the tough culture of construction. Tom creates connections and empathy through the stories he tells… He cares deeply about the safety, health, and wellbeing of all workers.

Cal Beyer, CWP; CSDZ, a Holmes Murphy Company.
National Workplace Advocate for Mental Health, Suicide
Prevention and Wellbeing. Executive Committee member at
National Action Alliance for Suicide Prevention

Tom is a true professional and brings a unique perspective to the construction industry that has been needed and overlooked for many years. There is a lot of focus and training in construction on how to do the "work" and "safety rules", but no one is talking about how to communicate and hold each other accountable. We have failed to train our industry on how to feel comfortable communicating up the chain of command, receiving that communication in a positive manner, and holding each other accountable. Tom's book is a must read for anyone in our industry who wants to improve their safety program.

Nick Davies, VP, EZ Excavating

CONTENTS

Intro to Book..11

Your Revolutionary Safety Plan.....................19

Safety Accountability and Teamwork.............29

Your Safety Mindset..33

When You See Something, Say Nothing..........37

Why So Reluctant to Speak Up?.....................43

The Courage to Speak Up................................49

Rank, Power and Accountability.....................53

What Construction Companies Can Learn
from Airplane Crashes....................................65

Put on Your Big Boy Pants!............................77

How to Train Your Reptilian Brain.................83

Build Trust by Admitting Mistakes
and Cleaning Up Messes.................................91

The Power of a Fake Apology.........................97

Courageous Conversations:
A Requirement for Safety Accountability.......107

Improve Your Communication Game:
Use the Feedback Loop..................................115

Giving Verbal Feedback in a Group Setting....121

Holding Others Accountable Can
Upset the Status Quo.....................................127

Personal Integrity the Keystone for Trust.......131

The Impact of the Man Box Culture...............143

Conclusion...153

Appendix..155

Dedication

I want to dedicate this book to my father, Greg Esch, one of my greatest teachers. And to Michael Esch, my uncle, who continued the family tradition in construction supplies after the 1969 fire at Otto N. Esch Equipment Supply Company. And to all those in construction who have challenged me, shaped me and mentored me. In particular, my brother Dan Esch, President and owner of Esch Construction Supply, LLC.

Note on photos: most of the photos in this book have been purchased and are being used with permission from www.depositphotos.com. A few are owned by the author and the black and white one in chapter fourteen, of Fr. Vito, was taken by Jeffry Jeaneatta-Wark and is being used w/permission.

INTRO TO BOOK

This is a book about communication, in particular the unwritten rules of communication as they relate to personal accountability and power. It is not about technical safety. Though much of my experience in construction is in the underground industry, I will say almost nothing about trenching safety or confined space safety or OSHA classes. Other than a few stories from my experiences training operators of demo saws, this is a book about the people-side of safety, which can revolutionize your business.

If you are as busy as I imagine you are, just read this six-point summary and you will understand the essence "personal accountability" from my point of view:

1. Personal accountability starts with you and your ability to build trust and keep your word.

2. Personal accountability goes beyond keeping the safety rules, though you and all your workers need to know and follow the rules.

3. Personal accountability happens when you have high personal integrity and are accountable for every part of your life. When you take extreme ownership of everything in your field of responsibility.

4. Personal accountability requires that you assess and manage the power dynamics and unconscious advantages (what some call "privileges") that you and others have in your company.

5. Personal accountability will ask you to commit to continuous personal improvement, including growing your capacity for effective communication. This means

expanding your emotional intelligence, becoming skilled at courageous conversations and building trusting relationships at work and at home.

6. Personal accountability will make you uncomfortable and upset the status quo and cause people to have emotional reactions. This is when the real work begins, not when it ends.

What is meant by "power"?

Power is a huge and diverse concept that is hard to nail down. There is "power over," "power with," "power by title," "the power to influence" and more. Please read chapters seven, *Rank, Power and Accountability* and eight *What Construction Companies Can Learn from Airplane Crashes* for specifics on what I mean by "power." See chapters four, *When You See Something, Say Nothing* and seventeen, *Personal Integrity the Keystone for Trust* for some of the "unwritten rules" of communication.

My limited perspective

I am aware that this book is written from my significant yet limited experience consulting, coaching, and training in the construction industry for the past twenty years. Almost all that work has been almost exclusively, at the owner, executive, and supervisory levels, with white men. Though I enjoy working with men and have learned many things from my clients, I wish for more diversity. Women bring valuable qualities and gifts that men need, especially when it comes to detailed communication and emotional intelligence. And people of color also bring value and perspective needed at this point in history, if this American experiment is going to survive and thrive. Plus, if you study population growth, Caucasians will be the minority population in less than 25 years. It is encouraging for me to see more women and people of darker skin colors coming into construction. The work of warmly welcoming, training and on-boarding them will not come easy to all of us.

Safety accountability

I refer to the combination of personal accountability and power as "safety accountability." It encompasses what you do and how you do it. Everyone in construction knows safety accountability is a good idea. Creating a workplace filled with highly accountable workers, who are excellent communicators and use their power to influence others skillfully, is good for business and good for safety. But how to build it into your culture? That is the question. This book will guide you to some answers. The work required to achieve a high level of safety accountability is not touchy-feely and it is not mumbo-jumbo. It is concrete and measurable. Developing this kind of culture requires incredible courage in certain moments, but most of the time you will find that the suggestions are achievable with the right focus, support systems and committed leaders.

The results you will see are inspiring if you stay the course. Following through on the roadmap laid out here will one day make a huge impact on your people and your bottom line. You can do some of this on your own, but depending on where you are starting, you will likely want outside support.

How did I get into this type of work?

My grandfather started Otto N. Esch Equipment Supply company in 1948 in St. Paul, Minnesota. He sold supplies to concrete contractors and others, many of whom had just come home from World War II. My father and my uncle grew up working in and eventually inherited that company. They had a tragic fire in 1969 which led my dad out of the business. My uncle Michael Esch stayed in the business and started a new company, later hiring my brother Dan Esch.

As a boy the things that interested me were not screwdrivers and hammers, but rather bats, balls and gloves. My original dream was to play professional baseball. My grandpa once said, "One of my grandkids will play pro ball." I believed him. My Uncle George had been drafted by the Yankees in the 1950s. Plus, my father was doing sports psychology back in the early 1970s with the Minnesota Twins, Minnesota Vikings, and other professional teams. Tony Oliva (Twins), Stu Voigt (Vikings) and other athletes came to our home for dinner. They told me what my dad was telling them: "You can do what you dream, Tom. Just imagine it and work hard!" I thought, "Yes, I can," and I have pretty good baseball genes. I did well in high school, played part of one year in college and then realized I did not have the physical strength to hit with enough power to keep the dream of being pro alive. It was NOT me!

About 25 years later my nephew, Jake Esch, was being compared to professional baseball star Joe Mauer in high school here in Minnesota. He became a star player at Georgia Tech and was drafted by the Miami Marlins after his junior year. He worked his way up to the big leagues and got his first start, as a pitcher, against the Mets in Met Stadium in New York city. It was a pretty big deal for him and for our family. He went on to pitch in several other games before moving on to the San Diego Padres and eventually decided to retire early. So, Gramps was right, just off by one generation.

My backup plan was to become a Catholic priest, go to Africa as a missionary and follow in the footsteps of Gandhi. I did become a priest and I did live in Africa. However, my vocation didn't last long. I realized that, though I loved the work, I could not live the lifestyle with integrity. Let's just say I passed preaching but flunked celibacy! Leaving that world was the hardest thing I've ever done. I wanted to minister but I also wanted to be married and have a family. I did marry a few years after leaving the priesthood, a wonderful woman whom I knew in high school and college. We have been married 22 incredible years.

The opportunity to get into the construction supply business happened in 2001, when I found myself semi-employed just a few months after our son Elijah was born. My brother Dan was willing to take on a significant risk—me, running a warehouse of supplies. Perfect for a former man of the cloth—operating a forklift, dealing with shipping, arranging commercial shelving and figuring out how to categorize, store and manage thousands of parts. Hey, Jesus was a carpenter, wasn't he? So perhaps it wasn't that far of a leap.

It only took a few fiascos in the warehouse—an incident involving the forklift and the garage door that I still can't quite talk about, and then my decision to take the plastic wrappers off of 500 tins of cashews. Right about then I got a promotion out of the warehouse and into the sales department. Brilliant decision, Dan.

I enjoyed many things about selling supplies and the tremendously good people I met in the construction industry.

Years later, the darkest day for me happened when I learned that an operator suffered a fatal injury using a demolition saw and a blade I had sold to his company. He died shortly after a pipe pinched on his blade and the saw kicked back on him. I wondered if I had done anything wrong. I knew I had followed all the right guidelines, but I worried that perhaps I had recommended the wrong blade, or that he was using the wrong saw, or a faulty saw, for the application. After all the OSHA investigations, it turned out that I had sold him the right blade for the job he was doing, and the saw was working properly. And yet some questions haunted me: Why did it happen? And how could it have been prevented?

I thought, "I used to be a Catholic priest. Now a construction worker was killed by tools I sold his company." This was disturbing. So, Dan, his marketing team and I put our heads together and created a demo saw-safety program that became one of the best in the country. It was rooted in a lot of learned experience, plenty of real-life stories and three generations of in-field expertise with the tools.

In a six-year span I trained over 8,000 operators of those saws.

This means I was one of the most active safety trainers in the country for demolition saws. In the process, I gathered plenty of stories about injuries—their causes, and how to prevent them. And many bloody pictures of injured workers. Workers with deep cuts to their legs, shoulders, chests, faces and necks.

One of the things I learned in training thousands of operators is that technical expertise is essential when using power tools in construction, but it is not enough. Cutting technique, proper ergonomics, knowledge of the tools and a basic understanding of physics are important to avoid injuries—but these are not enough. Awareness of hazards, excellent communication skills and having a positive attitude are all part of first-class safety.

I noticed that the companies that had better accountability, demonstrated better communication and practiced better mutual respect reported fewer injuries. Companies where workers were negative and rude to each other, places that lacked mutual respect, reported more injuries. I recall the specific company I was doing training for when this became obvious.

The leader was up in front of about 65 men, about to introduce me. The guys were talking and joking about him in a very mean-spirit way. I understand that men in construction have a way of relating to each other that can feel disrespectful to an outsider. I also know there is a line between playful joking and mean disrespect. This was on the mean side. He swore at a few of them. They yelled back at him. It felt dirty and ugly. Even a bit dangerous. I knew it would be a real trick to get them to listen to me and respect what I was saying. This company had an unusually high number of injuries and near misses from demo saws. Equally important, some of their key tenured leaders had a cavalier attitude about injuries and a lack of willingness to consider making changes to prevent those injuries. They said things like "You can't fix stupid Tom" and "These guys are idiots." Several men in the audience had scars from blades that had cut them on their faces.

I began to pay more attention to work culture and injuries. I connected the dots. It became crystal clear to me: places with a more positive work culture, where workers tended to treat each other with respect, were reporting fewer injuries. Places with more interpersonal conflict and "people problems" had more trouble with people getting hurt. Go figure.

So, a vital part of any safety solution is the task of building respect and accountability into your work culture. And it starts with improving communication. This is the main premise of this book. And it is not rocket science. It is people science. It is the science of communication.

Here are the core ideas behind this book: **work culture and safety accountability will improve as communication improves, and you will have fewer personnel issues and not as many injuries. As you take care of the people-stuff you will realize a more productive business. And the rules that govern the people-stuff are largely unwritten and not talked about much.**

Often, because of lots of good reasons and plenty of dumb excuses, we do not practice good communication skills. This is especially true in construction. And this leads to a breakdown in accountability and problems with safety.

You will learn things in this book that will make your jobsite safer and your work quality better and your company more profitable.

Let the brave, revolutionary work begin.

CHAPTER ONE

Your Revolutionary Safety Plan

"Give me six hours to chop down a tree and I will spend the first four sharpening the axe." —Abraham Lincoln

This book is about rising up and creating a revolution in your company: sharpening your axe and taking safety to a higher level in your business for the sake of the well-being of your greatest assets—your people—and for the profitability of your company. And it is also about chopping down.

My guess is that if you are reading this you have already invested in your people, but perhaps are not fully satisfied with the results. Is communication a problem for you? Retention? Attraction? Profitability? Safety?

Are you feeling pretty good about your safety culture? Is your experience modification rate (EMR) below average? Perhaps you have not had a really serious injury for a long time. Knock on wood. No deaths either. Good for you. Or maybe your EMR is not so great and you have had some serious injuries. Possibly even a death. Now you are truly motivated to change things in your company. Whatever your current situation, we can agree that even the companies with the best safety records can rise up to the challenge of improving their formal and informal systems to create a safer workplace.

For a very small number of companies, zero injuries is the goal. Like for the aluminum giant Alcoa, who had about 14,000 workers on duty when CEO Paul O'Neill gave one of the most riveting, controversial and sober safety speeches ever in June of 2015 at an investor meeting in New York. Alcoa had logged a few tough years in a row. He was being very brave when he said, "Every year, numerous Alcoa workers are injured so badly that they miss a day of work. . .I intend to make Alcoa the safest company in America. I intend to go for zero injuries."

Moving toward zero injuries is radical concept and one that lots of people will argue with. Regardless of what you believe about "zero" or Paul O'Neill, you have to agree he made safety accountability a top priority for his company. And his work paid off in multiple indicators. Just saying the word "zero" is like starting a fight for some. According to David Burkus, one of the world's leading business thinkers, O'Neill deliberately picked this fight, "He picked a fight with the idea that something inside the company was injuring and even killing their employees. O'Neill picked a fight with the notion that industrial manufacturing came with an 'acceptable' amount of risk. O'Neill wanted to fight the idea that any risk—any injury—was acceptable. He got to work recruiting others to join him in that fight." (see www. DavidBurkus.com, "How Paul O'Neill Fought for Safety at Alcoa," April 2020). According to Burkus, O'Neill also once said, *"Part of leadership. . .is to create a crisis."*

Safety accountability implies that individuals are taking responsibility for their own behavior and making changes when needed. And in cultures where people are not taking responsibility as often as they think they are, this will cause a crisis.

This crisis will include far more than the technical safety requirements. The manufacturers recommendations, the OSHA rules and your standard operating procedures are a starting point, and important to follow, but not the end game. The way that your people communicate, the manner in which they ignore or resolve conflict and the personal integrity they live by matters when it comes your safety culture. And these ways of interacting include individual and cultural behavior.

Individual behavioral change happens regularly. Sometimes it is relatively easy, and sometimes it is more difficult. With the right motivation and discipline, workers can quit taking shortcuts, laborers can start wearing their PPE every single time it is required, and everyone can change their phone habits while driving. People who rarely speak up can learn to speak up. Those who never initiated a candid conversation can start having several a week, with the right training. Personal change is possible, especially for people who have enough pain to warrant the energy that change requires.

Cultural behavioral change is *not* relatively easy, especially in cultures that prize individuality and freedom, as we tend to do here in the United States. There may be days or weeks when it happens naturally, and plenty of other times when it feels like climbing Mount Everest. Moving from a cultural norm of poor communication to one where people communicate well will take regular effort for an extended period of time. Improving the level of interpersonal accountability at your place of work, especially in regard to safety-related behaviors, will not come naturally. Getting foremen to have successful crucial conversations with others, if that currently rarely happens, can be a real pickle. How challenging these changes will be for you will depend on your current situation, the attitudes of the leaders and the skill level of your outside support professionals.

In order to rise up, you may have to first chop down. We who have been in construction for most of our lives tend to believe "If it ain't broke, don't fix it" and "Let sleeping dogs lie." Some of this common wisdom needs to be taken down. You may have to cut down the illusion that you have nothing to change. This book is also an invitation to stop and breathe before you do anything. Look in the mirror at yourself and your company. It could be that the way you are currently finding and training in workers needs an overhaul. You might discover that some of your workers need to find another place to work. You may have to chop down the old "cherry tree" in your own front yard that is keeping your apple and pear trees from thriving. You are good with tools. You can do what is needed. It requires the commitment and skill required to properly sharper your axe. And it involves telling the truth, even when doing so is difficult.

Just because you have not had a death or a maiming at your company does not mean you are doing all you can. If you have a great safety record, the ever-present danger is complacency. If you are hiring many workers who are not familiar with construction work, you have new exposure to risks and incidents. If you have a poor safety record, you may think that all those injuries are just part of the cost of doing business. The odds are good that there are some things that need to change for you to reach a maximum level of safety and profitability.

Some owners are very involved and hands-on with their workers. Others are hands-off and let the winds of chance shape their destiny. Some strike just the right balance of involvement and delegation. I know an owner who had a worker who was killed on a job. Sometime after that tragic event, he asked me to do my "Building a Culture of Safety Accountability" program for his company. I noticed that he didn't show up for the program I gave, which was aimed at holding everyone accountable to a higher standard of safety. What do you think of that?

Some trees are very hard. They need a super-sharp axe. This book is a way to sharpen your axe.

If you take the advice of this book you could become the source that leads to preventing life-debilitating injuries and deaths. Many companies that have gone on this kind of journey report real successes. Others report attempts they made that did not fully mature or that completely failed.

Just like every construction project you embark upon, you need to start with a plan—one that includes sufficient assessment, measurable goals and a timeline for monitoring progress, along with regular training and coaching input from a knowledgeable source outside of your business.

Your Plan

The first step is finding someone who has been down this road. This road of improving personal accountability and the way your people use power is filled with potholes and risks of various shapes, so you will want to talk with someone who understands where those hazards are and how to navigate the journey. And you will want to find someone who understands construction culture, which by its nature makes people development very challenging. You will need to lay out a vision for this project, identify the main purpose and set some preliminary goals. And almost always it is better that this person comes from outside of your organization.

The second step is to identify a group of internal leaders who can help guide the process. Some of these will be formal leaders (president, CEO, director of operations, superintendents) and some will be informal leaders (foremen, front-line workers and office staff who have a strong work ethic and a willingness to speak up respectfully). The group should not be too large. Three is too few, but ten is too many. I have no idea how Jesus managed twelve.

The third step is to create the time and space for your preliminary planning. You will need at least two half-days, and maybe more, to lay out the initial vision. I know companies that have taken three full days to make their plans to rise up to a new level. If you want more clarity and success take more time at the beginning. If you enjoy floundering around then take less time. How you begin, and the time required, depends on where your starting point is: If you have a clear and effective organizational structure with a high degree of business functionality, and individuals who generally communicate well, and have a strong levels of personal integrity, you will probably need less time; if you have an unclear structure with leaders who do not have strong interpersonal skills and may lack integrity in some areas of their lives, the process will take longer.

You may be tempted to minimize planning time. You are so busy completing jobs or finding new work. This is a common way in which contractors fail to prepare in doing this kind of work. If you can't give this the right amount of time right now, then wait until you can. Just realize that there will never be a perfect time for this kind of work. You will want to choose a time of the year when you can break away from the grind of daily work to talk with a mix of key leaders. If you do not have a slower season, then consider bringing on staff to fill some of the gaps or—imagine this crazy idea—taking on slightly less work for a few months to generate more time for planning.

The Consultant/Facilitator

Do not try to do this all by yourself. When addressing issues as potent as personal responsibility and power you will need assistance. Do not have your head of HR facilitate this, or your VP of Operations, or your owners. Bring in an outside, experienced professional: someone with education and expertise in organizational change; someone who can manage conflict and has positive energy and a sense of humor. Would you have your accountant fill in for your mechanic? Would you have your backhoe operator do your payroll? Get the round peg in the round hole. There are plenty of good facilitators out there. An experienced facilitator, with an understanding of organizational change within construction, is well worth their fee.

Measurable Goals

Some people say that you cannot set goals related to human behavior. They say that culture change is not measurable. Or that so called "soft skills" are too fuzzy to take stock of. Soft skills are poorly named, because they are perhaps the hardest skills of all, except maybe hitting a 101-mph low-tailing fastball. Of course, you can set goals related to human behavior—you just need to know what you are measuring and how to best measure it. You will need to set some benchmarks to begin with, in order to measure the changes later. Here are some things you can measure via a survey:

- How often are your people having the crucial conversations needed to keep relationships healthy and workers safe?

- Are all your crews doing a thorough, daily job hazard analysis (JHA) or job safety analysis (JSA)? Some also call this an A.C.E. (Access, Converse and Eliminate) drill.

- Would you say that your workers use an effective feedback loop (three-way communication) when communicating about important job details all the time, most of the time, about half the time, sometimes, rarely or never?

- On a scale of 1 to 5, with 5 representing highest level of trust, how high is the trust in your on-site foreman? Managers? Owners?

- How do you handle a worker who does not follow your directions?

- When you make a communication mistake, do you admit it all the time, most of the time, some of the time, rarely or never?

- When someone breaks a safety or company rule, how consistently is that situation handled by leaders?

- On a scale of 1 to 5, with 5 being the most proactive, how proactive are your leaders when it comes to addressing brewing conflict between workers?

Sharpen the Axe

Old honest Abe Lincoln would spend 66% of his time sharpening his axe. Four hours. What was he using, 100-grit sandpaper? It should take maybe 15 minutes, Abe! But my critique misses the point. Take the time required to plan and review, even if it feels substantial, to improve your odds of success.

What is axe sharpening in the world of safety accountability? It is planning, training, coaching and giving feedback to each other on the quality of your communication. It is talking with the person who is creating negative situations on their crew, and it is leaders using their influence to help that person see the value in taking a different approach. It is also making sure you have the right people in the right seats on the bus.

Timeline for the full process of culture change

How long should all of this take once you have a plan? It depends on where you are beginning from, how badly you want the changes to stick, and how quickly your leaders can align behind the purpose of the changes. A seasoned professional can help you set some rough timelines. This work is not like building a pole barn. You cannot bang this out in a few weeks or even a couple of months. Many people in the culture-change business say three to five years if you really want to get your business-ship headed in a different direction, but I don't mean to scare you. I have documented positive signs in as little as six months. I have seen systemic positive changes happen in as little as two years. Remember, if you change course even two degrees, you will be in a very different place when you reach your destination. And usually, you should see some hopeful signs happening in as little as six months if you are doing it right.

Where are you going?

Yogi Berra once had a good answer: *"If you don't know where you are going, you'll end up someplace else."* Brilliant wisdom, Yogi! Take the time to set your direction. Shaping the vision is one of your main jobs as a leader. Make sure you know where you are going. Create a plan and execute. This will involve chopping down and rising up. Culture change in the interest of safety accountability is a worthy journey that will improve your bottom line if done properly and sustained over time.

CHAPTER TWO

Safety Accountability and Teamwork

afety accountability is a team sport. You cannot do this alone. Your revolutionary plan will require working together closely with others, listening, influencing, and negotiating with them. Yet many of us in construction like to work alone and not be bothered. Do you prefer to do it your own way? Does asking for help seem like a sign of weakness to you? Do you have a hard time trusting the advice of others? Being raised in a family with strong military and Catholic values I have learned to do many things on my own. Asking for support and assistance is almost never my first move. To achieve five-star safety accountability, we all need to work as a team. Here is a story of how I once decided to be a team player and what happened as a result.

One fall I went fishing in northern Wisconsin with my son Elijah. He was just starting college and he loves to fish.

I wanted one last trip with him before the weather turned cold. That morning I caught a 44-inch musky, the fish of 10,000 casts, on the first cast of the day. What are the odds? Perhaps 1 in 10,000. How did I do it? Pure luck? Not exactly. I had an amazing team behind me.

We were planning to fish deep, clear, glacial lakes, and I knew that these kinds of lakes are challenging to fish. So, I started with Davey, a friendly fellow from Omaha who is a serious tournament fisherman. He recommended four lures for bass and crappie, and he even drew pictures of each one. I went off that night to buy them at the local Bass Pro Shops store. They only had one lure that was *exactly* what he recommended. All the rest were either 1/16th of an ounce off or a slightly different color. Davey was not happy with my purchases, except for one lure—the green pumpkin, paddle-tail 4-inch worm on a black ¼-ounce jig head that was perfectly matched to what he advised.

I also got some advice from a guy named Erik. He said something I had never thought of: *"If it is a tough lake to fish, Tom, get a guide."* So, even though I had to swallow my pride and get out my wallet, I took his advice and got a guide. He had over 500 exact fishing hotspots marked on his depth finder on just that one lake. His boat was old, his car was old, his fish finder was old, and his knowledge of the lake was old. Which is just what you want. His name is Tom Rice, and I highly recommend him if you are ever in the Cable/Hayward, Wisconsin area.

The first stop: a submerged tree, where he knew there were crappies suspended at 10-14 feet. He was giving my son his favorite crappie lure as I made my first cast. I had the 4-inch green pumpkin, paddle-tail worm on an eight-pound test line. A fish hit three seconds after my lure hit the cool, gray water. It felt like a good-sized walleye. I said, *"Nice... feels like a walleye, maybe 5 to 6 pounds."* That was because it was swimming toward the boat. The guide watched as the fish moved quickly towards the boat. My pole bent and the fish went down deep. Fortunately, I had my drag set perfectly for this kind of fish. He said, *"That's a musky."* *"No way!"* I replied. What felt like 30 minutes later, we somehow landed the monster. The line broke as the fish fell into the boat. My son got it all on video and took several pictures. Sixty seconds later, the fish was back in the water. It was the happiest moment of my fishing life.

And it took a full team to get me there: Davey, the staff at Bass Pro Shops, Erik, Tom our guide and my son Eli to film it.

Do you tend to be a cowgirl or cowboy? Do you prefer to go it alone? Is it hard for you to trust others? I tend to be that way. But not this trip. I decided to take help and trust the support and advice from a team of people who know fishing. . It took that team along with my fairly basic ability to cast, set my drag and reel in the fish, to put that 44" beast in the boat.

When it comes to safety accountability, what are you doing alone that you could be doing with a team? Where does your ego get in the way? In which kind of situations is trusting others a challenge for you? What tasks are you doing now that could use a little more teamwork? Are you delegating enough? Are you trusting others? Are you getting the results you want?

Here is my challenge to you as a fellow cowboy or maybe cowgirl: open up to being more of a team player. Consider that you need support and if you want to understand your leadership style, including areas where you can improve, you will also need feedback. You, and your people, will be less likely to be injured as you work together more effectively. You will be more likely to feel as if you are making a difference and you just might land the biggest "fish" of your life.

CHAPTER THREE

Your Safety Mindset

Accountability begins with mindset. Awareness of your mindset.

Downhill skiing was one of my top passions in high school. It is a sport full of hazards and we knew that bad things, like spinal cord injuries, sometimes happened to good skiers. I don't recall ever noticing a younger person in a wheelchair, until my senior year. We did what they called "freestyle skiing." My brothers, our friends and I did jumps, tricks and had all kinds of adventures on the slopes. Our mindset was simple: "We are invincible!" We thought we would never get injured, and for the most part, we never were. We built a ski jump, as well as a ramp to give us more speed, in our backyard. Each year it got bigger and attracted more attention. We went from doing 360 helicopter jumps, to front and back flips. I was the first to successfully complete a full backflip. It was the most exciting thing I'd ever done in my life up to that point! We knew the risks; we knew some skiers had broken their necks and backs. I was sure it would never happen to me. Do you know anyone like that in construction?

And then it happened. Some friends came over to see the jump and to watch me do flips. I was showing off. Laid it out beautifully, slowly. It felt perfect, until I landed right on my head. It does not take that much force to sever a spinal cord. A 12-foot fall onto your head is plenty of force to break your neck. I know, because mine was broken—a fracture in my C5 vertebra. Lucky for me, it was a minor fracture, and the spinal cord was intact. I wore a neck brace for several weeks and dealt with pain and went to chiropractors for some years. Eventually it healed. Thank God I did not sever my spinal cord, because I would have instantly been a quadriplegic. That was the day I started noticing people in wheelchairs and the last day I tried a backflip in the backyard.

My mindset changed that day. What is a mindset? It is the way your mind is set on a given topic. Kind of like a filter. We have mindsets about all kinds of things. Maybe you like watching NFL football, maybe you don't, but you probably have a mindset about pro football. You likely have a mindset on COVID-19: you may think it is overblown or under-blown, or maybe your mindset is moderate or undecided. Undecided, too, is a mindset.

I went from "It won't happen to me." to "It could happen to me." and I changed my behavior. I still skied and did some jumping; I just stopped doing back flips. Can you change your mindset before you are injured? That is a good question.

Here are three keys to understanding and controlling your mindset that I use when working with construction workers:

#1. Admit that you may not be fully aware of your mindset because of the nature of mindsets. You do not know what you do not know. This seems so obvious I feel stupid saying it. Mindsets are kind of like slightly tinted safety glasses. When you first put them on, you see the yellow tint—the filter. But after about five minutes, you don't notice the tint. Similarly, it is possible you do not see your safety mindset clearly, until some big event happens.

#2. Realize that you can trick yourself; you can say, "Oh, yes, I have a strong mindset on being COVID compliant. I am 100% on board." But then you only wear your face mask and abide by the 6-foot rule half the time. You are not 100% compliant; you are 50% compliant. You just *think* you are 100% compliant, maybe because you think you *should* be that way.

Some may say, "Oh, yes, I'm 100% committed to safety." But then they do some things that do not match that statement: they use a power tool above their shoulders; they don't put out the traffic cones properly; they do not put shoring up on a 5' 1" deep trench. Watch your behaviors to understand your mindset. Behavior rarely lies.

Also, ask others for honest feedback. That is another way to discover whether your self-perception is accurate. We all have blind spots. It is likely that you do too.

#3. Understand that you can change your mindset with the right motivation—mindsets are not locked in stone or permanent. They seem that way, because we defend them strongly. We would rather *not* change—it is normative human behavior to want to stay the same—but we *can* change.

It is not my goal here to change your mindset on safety. In fact, another person cannot change your mindset. Only you can do that. It sometimes takes a traumatic event, a serious injury or a near-death experience for us to begin to see our mindsets and to consider changing them. Or it might just take some concrete feedback from someone we trust, a sensible committed decision and the proper support. This is the work of culture change, and accountability, creating an environment where your workers could talk to each other honestly about things like their safety mindset and change them before the serious accident.

Your mindset around safety is a matter of personal choice. The potential impact of your personal choices is a matter of public record. What you do or do not do affects other people. The key is to be aware of your mindset and open to feedback from others. What you think about safety will determine how engaged you are in the way you work and the risks you take. It is very important to accurately understand your own mindset to be as safe as possible.

Even more important is to create the sort of work culture where people are transparent about their mindsets and able to influence each other by their example and conversations.

There is a tendency in the construction world for people to say nothing. To not speak up. We will look at this pervasive problem in the next chapter.

CHAPTER FOUR

When You See Something, Say Nothing

After the terrorist attacks of 9/11 in New York and Washington, DC, in the interest of national safety, we began to develop some new ways of looking out for each other. We put up signs in and near airports that say, "If you see something, say something." It is good advice anywhere, but especially at an airport or a jobsite. It is good advice because speaking up takes courage, plus not all people are motivated to speak up, especially when something not quite right is going on. When something not quite right is going on some of us get very quiet. Occasionally there is that worker who speaks up, but sometimes they are too vocal, or too abrasive and this isn't helpful either.

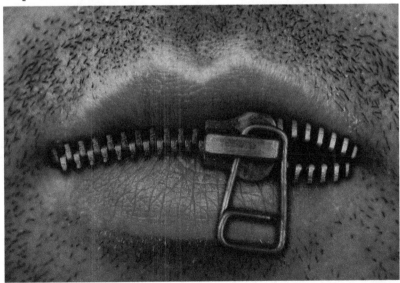

One of the common communication problems in construction involves this problem of workers getting quiet at the wrong time.

Both field workers and others who have higher-level positions are sometimes reluctant to speak up, especially when it comes to safety.

There are dangerous moments every day, somewhere, when speaking up is demanded by the circumstances. There are lots of well-documented reasons why workers in most companies do not speak up when someone is doing something unsafe, especially if the person doing the risky thing is someone of higher positional or social rank. But every owner, every safety leader wants their field workers to speak up. To anyone, anytime. And many of them act as if they believe that saying "Come on, guys, speak up anytime you see something unsafe!" will cause them to do so. Most often it will not. Laborers have all heard the mantra "When you see something, say something." In most construction work cultures workers see lots of things; many of them say almost nothing.

Unfortunately, sometimes those unspoken words allow accidents and even deaths to happen. I know the details of several such incidents. One happened on a jobsite not long ago, where there was a 30-foot-deep trench. The job had multiple challenges— heavy traffic, electrical considerations and schedule pressures. The leaders did a good job of pre-planning and making sure all the risks were identified and hazards mitigated. There was a lot of good communication beforehand.

As they were finishing, they had several trench boxes to retrieve from the hole. They agreed ahead of time to not go down into the trench to retrieve the rigging, but instead to use machinery to haul it up. At the last possible moment, a crew leader decided to go down and adjust some of the rigging by hand. Another worker went with him. At least ten workers were close enough to the situation that they could see what was happening. They all knew that what these two were doing was not according to plan and was a serious safety risk. No one spoke up.

As everyone in the business knows, it is not uncommon for leaders to change a project plan in the interest of efficiency.

Also, it is common for workers to keep to themselves and not intervene in the tasks of others. These two factors can be like a match set to a keg of dynamite. Some men get into construction precisely because it is possible to work a full day and have very little conversation. And it is relatively rare for anyone to interrupt the work you are doing, especially if you are seasoned or have high status.

Shortly after the men went down in the trench there was a catastrophic collapse of earth. A single cubic yard of soil weighs an astounding 4,000 pounds—about the weight of a small pickup truck. The leader was able to escape. The other worker was buried in many tons of earth. The workers began frantically searching for him. They could not find him in time. He was crushed to death by the weight of the soil. Take a minute to let that one soak in. Never again will he see his kids, his wife, his friends. Gone. Permanently. May his soul and the souls of all the faithfully departed, through the mercy of God, rest in peace. Amen.

Something like this happens every day on jobsites in America. The one in charge does it the way they want to or changes the plan to something riskier. Perhaps in the interest of productivity or cost-savings. People see what he is doing. Everyone wants to save time. Owners want to save money. No one wants to suffer negative feedback from the boss. No one wants to look foolish. So, no one speaks up.

When the workers who were at the site that day were interviewed, many said something like this: *"I knew what we were doing was wrong, but I didn't say anything."* Can you imagine being the one who went to tell the wife of the worker who died that he would not be coming home? I know that man. It was a very difficult day for them all.

That is the bad news. The good news is that this particular death was the prime motivator behind an inspiring resource. The "Speak Up! Listen Up!" program was spearheaded by Caterpillar, along with a group of contractors, after this death in the trenching accident. It was released in 2007 and has since been translated into many languages and delivered to thousands of companies. It has contributed to workers both speaking and listening more courageously. Who knows how many lives have been saved? Brilliant job by Caterpillar and the companies who backed the creation of this program.

The only critique I have of "Speak Up! Listen Up!" is that they do not address the important issue of rank. They offer good advice on speaking up and listening, but do not cover the reasons why speaking up is so difficult, especially in construction, and they do not offer strategies to mitigate those challenges.

One of the unwritten rules of communication in male-oriented work cultures is that person with lower seniority is not supposed to speak up to a higher-ranked person. Unless you have done the right training in your workplace to change those cultural rules, or have an unusually outspoken worker, and this rule will be consistently enforced.

Another unwritten rule is the flip side, that if you have higher seniority you do not need to listen to someone of lower rank. This can be a significant problem and a subtle but important thing you need to change to rise up to a new level of safety accountability.

The keys to changing workforce cultural rules and norms are contained in this book: committed leadership, personal integrity, trust, communication tools and an understanding of how seniority (also called rank) and power impact healthy work culture.

The main points from this true story are related to seniority and communication:

- It is very challenging in the male-oriented construction world for workers to speak up to others in the interest of safety.

- Seniority, or positional rank, can impact speaking up and safety in male-oriented cultures.

- It is possible to change the culture and arrive at a different ending to this story. It involves making it emotionally safe and expected to speak up, and making sure others listen up—especially those of higher seniority.

- This task of making it emotionally safe is more challenging than it first appears.

The best and most profitable construction companies do what it takes to minimize the seniority factor when it comes to safety.

Minimizing the force of rank unwritten rules of seniority and maximizing the capacity of workers to speak up respectfully will require communication training, professional coaching and a strong vision. A senior safety leader cannot do it alone. A superintendent or even a group of foremen cannot do it. Since these changes are systemic and alter deeply imbedded male-cultural norms, leaders from the top, guided by outside support, have to drive these changes.

If the lower-ranked worker would have gone down into the trench, against the plan, would the superintendent have spoken up and stopped him? Quite possibly. If either had gone down into the trench at a company where workers had the tools and support to speak up, that person would not have died that day.

Perhaps you are beginning to see something at your company from a different angle. Is there something for you to say? To whom do you to speak with to move the ball on this important topic? You can be a force for igniting the conditions for change that could prevent injuries and save lives. What are a few areas in your workplace that need more speaking up? And do your leaders, including you, need to listen better?

CHAPTER FIVE

Why So Reluctant to Speak Up?

One day in 1978, a pilot named Malburn McBroom was flying a United Airlines plane that was supposed to land at an airport in Portland, Oregon. According to those who knew him and have since studied the crash, McBroom had quite a temper, and people feared him. He was someone you just didn't mess with, and people worked hard not to make him angry.

On this flight, they had to go into a holding pattern because of an issue with the landing gear. Captain McBroom was quite upset about solving the landing-gear issue. The issue was not being resolved, and they continued in the same holding pattern. The co-pilots were watching the gauges that indicated the fuel was getting lower and lower. From the recordings recovered later, it appears that they were afraid to interrupt McBroom. It is likely they were afraid because they had seen what he could do to people who interrupted him, especially when he was obsessed about something. *So, they did nothing. They were silent.* They just watched the gauges until the plane ran out of gas and crashed, killing ten people and injuring many.

You can read more details of this story in Malcolm Gladwell's outstanding book *Outliers* in chapter seven, "The Ethnic Theory of Plane Crashes." I refer you to it for more detail.

That tragic crash, and the reasons it happened, was the genesis for major changes in airline crewmember training. It helped to launch a new approach to safety in the cockpit, called "crew resource management" (CRM). See Wikipedia, "United Airlines Flight 173". United Airlines instituted the first CRM training for pilots in 1981. Some have called this accident the most important one ever in aviation history.

You might think *"How could these two co-pilots, in effect, choose death over speaking up?"* or *"Had I been the co-pilot I would have spoken up."* I'm not sure what I would have done. We know that one of the greatest human fears is public speaking. I would say an even more powerful fear is speaking up when it is likely that you will be verbally attacked for it. It generates an interest in silence. Your natural survival instincts, based in your brain, make silence seem like a reasonable choice. Deadly silence. And I believe this seemingly "reasonable choice" happens every day on construction sites all over America. This is another one of the unwritten rules of communication: do not speak up, especially to a higher ranked person with a temper!.

Why are we so afraid to speak up? And what can we do about it?

How often, at your place of work, has someone not said or done something important because of fear? Fear that they might lose their status. Fear of looking stupid. Fear of retaliation. Fear of conflict. Fear of an emotional outburst on the part of someone else. Fear of ultimately losing their job. And what is their inability to overcome that fear costing your company? What health and safety risks are you enduring because of people who lack the training to act and to do the right thing, despite their fear?

We are afraid to speak up because of the design of our brains and because we lack the training to counter its natural ways of protecting us. When we sense any threat whatsoever, big or small, the brain sends a signal to the body to get ready to fight to the death, or to flee, or to freeze. In the above case, it seems the two co-pilots froze. And ironically, the instinct for survival was exactly the thing that, from Gladwell's point of view, caused ten deaths and many injuries.

Since the invention of the functional MRI machine in the 1990s, we now know a lot about what happens in the brain when certain things occur. When a person senses a threat of any sort, the amygdala is engaged, and the prefrontal cortex area of our brain goes dark. That means that our logical-thinking functions are impaired. Then hormones are released into the bloodstream that allow us to act, the classic fight or flight. This is part of the survival design. Apparently, when one was attacked by a wooly mammoth or a saber-toothed tiger, rational thought was not considered as valuable as the more basic capacity just to kill (fight) or to run (flee) or to hide (freeze). This automatic response has served us well as a species when it comes to survival. But it does not always serve us well at work, especially when what our brain labels a "life threat" is just a person having a bad day and expressing some momentary anger. It is even more problematic when you are operating heavy machinery and having an emotional response to a threat, real or perceived. Your ability to think, and so to safely operate that equipment, is impaired. It is almost like you are drunk.

What if those two co-pilots had enough training to override their momentary fear of McBroom's anger? What if instead of being paralyzed, they were able to take deep breaths and engage their parasympathetic system, and then looking at the facts and taking logical action. They might have spoken up strongly and said *"Captain, the gauges show we are almost out of fuel; we need to land soon." "We must land in five minutes or we will crash!" "I know the landing gear isn't right, but we have a more urgent concern. You need to listen to us."* These should have been the messages McBroom's co-pilots gave him that day. If they had better emotional control and emotional intelligence, it is possible that they could have averted that deadly crash.

Have your workers ever left a jobsite or a meeting and said something like the following? *"Can you believe he said that?",*

"That idea will never fly.", "That is going to hurt profits." "Boy, he really threw Andy under the bus." or "She didn't deserve that!"

When we say things like this, we know something more productive could happen, but we do not say it. Sometimes we do not know what to say. Or we do not want to stir the pot. We are nervous about upsetting others and afraid of conflict. But as a result, we risk of burning the stew. We are all reluctant to say or do something that will rock the boat. But we need to stir pots and rock boats, in ways that are effective, to achieve the highest levels of safety accountability.

When your people know they should say something and they do not, you may be inadvertently contributing to a dangerous work culture. In avoiding conflict, we often make things worse later. The trouble grows, it rarely shrinks. And then the cleanup can be very costly in dollars and hours. According to *Forbes Magazine, "Conflict Resolution, When Should Leaders Step In," May 2014*, managers spend 10-25% of their time attempting to resolve conflict, as opposed to spending that time focused on the job. I personally think for many in construction management, this range is low.

Would you like to see more people speaking up, breaking the expensive silence that happens all too often?

If your answer is "yes," then I suggest three things:

1. Give your leaders training in how to modulate their amygdala (the part of your brain where the fight/flight/freeze response originates). It is a significant part of the reason they are not speaking up.

2. Grow your emotional intelligence. Yes, it is possible; your IQ is much harder to improve than your emotional intelligence (EI) quotient.

3. Consider contacting a consulting firm like Esch Consulting, LLC (www.EschConsulting.com) for support—you will need it.

This work is very doable. Lots of companies are figuring this out. It can be relatively easy if you get the right support. It will involve understanding and naming, and rewriting the unwritten rules around silence. You will have workers able to bravely speak up in a way that would help a guy like Malburn McBroom safely "land the plane." You will save lives *and* improve the bottom line of your business at the same time.

CHAPTER SIX

The Courage to Speak Up

Some of us were born in families and cultures where speaking up is the very last thing we would do, maybe just before death. Or maybe never. I was born in Minnesota, where we have perfected the art of not speaking up. But my family was a little different than most. Somehow, I developed the inner confidence to speak up. Often, I have not spoken up at the right time. And plenty of times I have not spoken up at all. And sometimes I've actually done it right at the moment when it was needed.

This is America. We prize our individuality and our own freedoms. This is especially true in construction and in the trades. Speaking up may imply asking another to examine or change their behavior. Who am I to ask you to change your behavior? Especially if you have seniority over me. And in a country that is more politically polarized now and better armed than perhaps ever before, speaking up can be risky business.

One day I saw something, and I said something. It took some courage. It happened in Omaha, Nebraska. An operator of a demo saw was lying prone, under the back end of a pickup truck near the shoulder of a busy two-lane road. He was holding his Stihl demo saw with one hand, with the diamond blade plunged in the asphalt at full depth. He had no PPE on, he was not cutting with water and the saw was shaking badly. He looked like he was about to injure himself. I could not remain silent. I stood at a safe distance and got the attention of the guy working next to him. He yelled at the saw man to stop. He shut the saw off and the man stood up facing me.

I happen to have a lot experience with these saws and with diamond blades, as I mentioned in the introduction to this book. I sold and promoted these saws and blades for 15 years, with Esch Construction Supply. The saw is portable and powerful, and the risks associated with it are, in my professional opinion, underestimated. And it is used improperly with great regularity.

So, when I saw this guy in Omaha lying face down on the tarmac, under a truck, holding a 14-inch Stihl Cutquick saw, with one hand I had to speak up! He stopped cutting and stood up after I got his attention. He looked at me in a way that indicated he would listen to me, so I spoke. *"Excuse me, sir, I have led a lot of safety trainings on handling that saw you are using and was watching you just now. Did you know that every year 10–15 operators in America are killed by the improper use of that saw?"* No answer. He seemed a little shocked that a stranger was speaking to him. *"You are safer when you hold it with two hands. You may want to pull the truck forward so you can use both hands on that tool and get more leverage."* He looked at me like he couldn't believe what I was saying. He said nothing. When I returned minutes later, I saw that he had not moved the truck. But he had put away the saw.

There are at least five reasons I was able to stop and engage this young man:

1. I was raised with enough confidence to speak up.

2. I have had professional training in how to use that confidence and be effective, some of the time, in moments just like this one.

3. I am very familiar with the tool he was using.

4. I am passionate about helping construction workers handle that tool safely.

5. I believe the things we say to each other, if said respectfully and skillfully, can make a difference and save lives.

How confident are you that your workers are willing and able to interrupt other workers respectfully, in the interest of safety? Can they get someone to stop doing what they are doing, and still maintain a positive relationship with that person?

A comment I hear, when a worker sees another doing something wrong, starts something like this: *"Hey, dumbass . . ."* This is neither respectful nor skillful. It might appear temporarily effective, but it is certainly not a communication best practice. And it will not engender trust or a healthy working relationship. If that is the way you or your co-workers speak, even some of the time, I believe you would agree there is some room for learning some other approaches.

It is common to ignore other workers, including the person a tool or piece of machinery above their shoulders. What you may hear are things like this: *"He'll learn the hard way"* and *"It's not my business."* How about when someone tells the lowest-ranking guy to go and cut the pipe or a section of concrete. The person may not have had any training on how to safely use the demo saw. And the one telling them may not ask, *"What training do you have on that tool?"* or *"When is the last time you used it?"* And it is possible that they don't speak good English and the person telling them does not speak their language. It is a rare construction worker who has the courage to admit that they do not know much about a tool, or that they do not feel comfortable running it.

There is a link between the courage to admit the truth and the number of reportable injuries. The way people trust and treat each other matters. I've trained in shops with 220 workers, where you could hear a pin drop. Complete respect. I've also trained at companies where there were 50 people in the room, and several were rudely cussing at the person who was introducing me and then talking while I was talking. Guess which places tend to have more injuries and near misses? Yes, naturally, the ones where people openly show disrespect at company meetings.

The risk of serious injury and death is lowered when workers respectfully interrupt each other when they see a problem. This is not a common practice at most of the construction companies where I have worked, yet every owner and safety person would like it to become a common practice. Everyone would be safer, and lives would be saved, if respectful interruptions happened more often.

Make sure that all your workers get the training they need to identify risky situations and to speak up with respect and confidence when they do. People can be taught how to speak up. It is easier than calling a spouse to give them the worst news of their life.

One of the most common and yet not discussed reasons that workers are reluctant to speak up, especially in male-dominated cultures with strong rules related to seniority, is rank. It is easy for an owner or executive leader to underestimate the power of rank and the difficulty of making it safe enough people to speak up. From your point of view, it looks easy. This is largely due to your rank. We will look at rank and how it impacts communication and safety culture in the next two chapters.

CHAPTER SEVEN

Rank, Power and Accountability

This may be the most important chapter in this book. It is about a topic that is ever present but rarely talked about in construction: rank. It is commonly understood as seniority, but the concept of rank has more dimensions. Specifically, we will discuss being aware of and accountable for your rank.

You may think of the military when I use the word "rank," and that is a good starting place. Construction cultures are not unlike the military with their hierarchy of authority and preponderance of male workers. Structured leadership, with clear roles, is necessary to safely get work done amid so many daily hazards. There is nothing inherently wrong with having or using rank. Unless it is misused or abused. Which tends to happen more than you might think.

My interest in rank and power started the day a good friend looked me in the eye and told me that my mentor had been sexually abusing women. It was one of the most disturbing things I had ever heard. I was in the seminary studying to be a priest, at the University of Notre Dame, in South Bend, Indiana. He was the one, back here in Minnesota, who inspired me to consider ministry as a priest. He impacted my life in many positive ways. He was a charismatic minister and friend, who had taken advantage of his privileges in ways that were unbelievable. She knew because many women had come to her to tell their story.

She was the one who went and courageously spoke up to the local bishop, beginning the process of ending his official ministry as a priest. Bravo! That was 1987. In the next three decades many similar stories became public, and abusive church leaders were stopped, as the force of law was applied to both Catholic and Protestant ministers, who misused and abused their rank.

When I got ordained I felt the visceral power of my rank. It felt good. People instantly trusted me. They deferred to my authority because of my status as a priest. It was a potent experience. Though I never followed in my mentor's dark footsteps, I understand how it happened. And I have forgiven him. It is challenging to be fully aware of the impact you have on others when you possess high rank. And it is not always easy to manage the many advantages which rank brings you.

Rank is present whenever human beings interact. Rank is an important part of day-to-day reality on every jobsite in America, though it is seldom talked about openly. When rank is talked about it is typically minimized or dismissed completely, especially by those with lots of it. I was recently working with a mid-sized company and we were discussing rank. One of the owners said, "We don't really have rank around here. We are all treated the same." Really?

Understanding rank properly, and how it functions when it comes to communication, will help you lower your risk of serious injuries and has the potential to improve your financial bottom line. Rank has an internal dimension, by virtue of personality and inner power. Do you know someone who is a janitor or common laborer but fearless about speaking up? Rank also has an external dimension, created by what the society or organization deems important. Rank is an often-underestimated part of safety and healthy work culture.

Few writers and thinkers have explored the concept of rank more than Dr. Arnold Mindell. He, along with his wife Amy and several others, founded the Process Work Institute in Portland, Oregon decades ago. I have been fortunate to spend years studying with him and his most experienced colleagues. Most of his work is outside of the construction industry, and so his language might feel somewhat foreign to you. That's ok though, because the concepts he is talking about are universally human and found in every business. Mindell has authored over 20 books on rank and similar topics. He defines rank simply as the *"sum of a person's privileges"* (Mindell, *Sitting in the Fire*, 1995, p. 28). He calls rank a *"conscious or unconscious, social or personal ability or power arising from culture, community support, personal psychology or spiritual power"* (Mindell, *Sitting in the Fire*, p. 42).

Rank has to do with privilege and power—specifically, how privilege influences human relationships and communication. Rank is not the same thing as power, but it is close. Rank is about how the benefits of privilege, or "unconscious advantage" are utilized and structured in social groups and professional organizations. Power is about the raw ability to influence behavior and change. For more on "unconscious advantage" a term coined by author and serial entrepreneur Anthony Signorelli, meant to distinguish how— especially for men— the word "privilege" tends to shut down a conversation, while the phrase "unconscious advantage" can keep the lines of communication open, see *Fielding the Hard Hit Ball Called "Privilege": A Guide for Men, May 2018*).

Years ago, while I was visiting my son's grade school, I had an opportunity to notice rank impacting an everyday situation. I was walking down the hall and saw a boy, about 5 years old, walking on his toes in an erratic fashion using a little walker. He was shouting down the hallway to an older child who was walking slowly toward him, *"Hurry up. Hurry up! Hurry up!!!"* he said. His tone was urgent and escalating. The other boy was taking his merry time. I watched for a few moments and then could not stand it. I was next to the boy walking slowly and I bent down to him and gently said, *"I think he wants you to hurry up."* After I said that, the boy began running toward the other child. This little scene was an example of rank in action. The slow-walking boy, being older and more physically able to move freely, probably had more positional rank than the other and did not feel a need to respond to the other's urgent shouts. However, as an adult, I had more rank than either, and it was easy to use my influence for the benefit of the boy with the disability. In this case, my request ignited a quick and proper response.

Four Types of Rank: Social, Positional, Psychological and Spiritual

This is a simple summation of Dr. Arnold Mindell's theory on the most common types of rank. Please note that rank is not a fixed-forever reality. It is ever changing as humans and social systems evolve. And at this point in history, because of the MeToo movement, the Black Lives Matter movement and even the impact of COVID-19, we are seeing shifts in the dynamics of power and rank. These shifts tend to be unsettling for those on top of the rank mountain and encouraging for those at the bottom.

There are many types of rank. Four of the most common types are worth mentioning here.

Social Rank

This form of rank is determined by the culture and society in which we live. It has more to do with the perceptions of others and less to do with one's personal choices. It includes the biases and prejudices of the mainstream society. Social rank bestows more privileges, or unconscious advantages, to some people and fewer advantages to others. Every society has certain things and kinds of people that are favored and have more rank. The culture of India has a caste system. African culture has tribalism. The Western world has racism. Many cultures are marked by sexism. These are all structures that shape social rank. In addition, social rank is shaped by the following:

- *Gender.* Your gender is an important part of your social rank. Gender is especially visible in construction, where 89.7% of all workers in the U.S. were male in 2019, according to www.Statistica. Though things are shifting on the topic of gender in the western world, most would agree that men are still given more social rank than women. If you doubt this, just look to men's and women's professional sports. Consider that in 2019-20 season Sue Bird, a top WNBA basketball player, earned a salary of $215,000 while NBA star LeBron James pulled in $37.44 million. Rank is not the only reason men are paid more in sports, but it is one part of the equation. Or listen to the experience of many women working in construction when largely outnumbered by men.

- *Economic class.* The more wealth one has, the more affluent the neighborhood one lives in, the larger the house, etc., the more social rank one is given.

- *Education.* Those who have attained higher levels of learning are given more rank and financial recognition.

- *Skin color.* In general, the lighter the skin, the more favorable the social rank.

- *Age.* Age is especially relevant in construction. If you are supervising men who are 10-20 years older than you it is going to be a challenge. In many western countries, the needs of older people and very young children are not well recognized. Youth is admired, and younger, sexier bodies have more rank.

- *Sexual orientation.* Heterosexuals are given more recognition, rank and support than people who identify as homosexual, bisexual or transgender. There may be some sub-cultures or isolated situations where this is not true, but for the most part the traditional standards of sexual orientation exist.

- *Health.* The healthier and more athletic one's body, the greater the rank. Those with differing or alternative abilities have lesser rank.

- *Physical strength.* The stronger you are, the more physical rank you have over others, especially in a group of men doing physical labor.

- *Mechanical expertise.* The guy who can operate machinery has higher rank on a jobsite than most others who can't. When I sold construction supplies, the guy in the warehouse who was best at running the forklift had higher rank than others who worked there.

Positional Rank

Positional rank is often partly given and partly earned. It is like social rank but places more emphasis on the influence of the context in which the interaction occurs. You can usually tell positional rank by the title of the person. The foreman has more rank than the part-time mechanic. The general superintendent has more positional rank than an on-site supervisor. The owner has more positional rank than the head of HR. In a small business, the owner may be a woman who is also a minority by virtue of her race. While she has lower social rank in at least two categories than the Caucasian men who work for her, she has higher positional rank because she has earned her way to the top. Her positional rank entitles her to specific advantages that others may not enjoy.

Like social rank, positional rank tends to be shaped by external factors, but not entirely. The parts runner who eventually becomes a skilled project manager and is then promoted to vice president of a mid-sized construction company has grown her positional rank because of her discipline, skill and performance. She is by nature hard-working, smart and emotionally intelligent. Her positional rank is both earned and given.

Psychological Rank

Those with high psychological rank can stay calm when others have their feathers ruffled. They are good to have in an emergency or during difficult meetings. These people have developed internal abilities, or have advanced training, that gives them greater personal comfort and ease in addressing challenging situations. Psychological rank tends to be more internally earned than externally given, which makes it quite different from social rank.

I know someone who has low positional rank in a company but is fearless in speaking up. He speaks up to his foreman, to the superintendent and even the executives. He has high psychological rank. He is not necessarily using his rank well, because he irritates those above him. He is at risk of being "the boy who cried wolf," or getting punched in the nose. But I do give him credit for doing what so many are afraid to do. He just needs some coaching to use his rank more productively. Using your rank well is not the same as having it.

Psychological rank can also be developed by those who experience lower social rank. I was discussing physical safety with an African American male friend. We were discussing the differences between the experience of some people of darker skin related to those who are white in social situations. He said that as an African American, he never felt safe in groups or in being stopped by police at night. He had developed what he called an inner "psychological-warrior energy" so that he could stay alert and watch out for himself in difficult social situations. Keeping alert and watching his own back was a psychological-rank practice he developed due to having less social rank.

Spiritual Rank

"Spiritual rank comes from a relationship to something divine or transcendent" (Mindell, *Sitting in the Fire*, p. 62). It can occur naturally through personal spiritual training, or because of having lesser social and psychological rank, or from surviving the painful experiences of life and remaining grateful and grounded. It comes from a connection to a divine power, or a transcendent state that creates a detachment and an experience of freedom outside of the wheel of ordinary life. Those with spiritual rank have a lot of inner power and an ability to bring calm in difficult times. They do not try to control others or convince others to follow a certain path. They can let go.

Do you know a worker who has spiritual rank? Someone who is like a steady anchor when the whole job has gone to the dogs three times over. My mom has high spiritual rank. She has lived through just about everything I can imagine: the end of the

Great Depression, the loss of her first child, raising five strong-willed children, and 84 Minnesota winters. She remains positive, funny, loving, grateful for just about everything, warm and tough. She has a special spiritual connection with God, and she has a powerful impact on others. She is empathetic and loved by many.

You may ask what spiritual rank has to do with construction. If you have high spiritual rank you will be naturally resilient. And with all of the dramatic and sometimes dangerous social, political and racial changes happening, you better have some key leaders who are spiritually grounded and can model resilience and calm in the face huge forces of change.

Do you feel you have high, low or medium rank in any of these four main areas? If you are not sure, think about the area and study the signs listed below. They may help you decide if you have high or low rank. These signs do not all need to be present for you to have high or low rank in any one category. Also, note that it is possible to have high rank, but use it poorly. This is bad for communication, for business and for safety.

Signs of High Rank

- interrupting others
- ignoring the requests of others
- feeling energized, important and/or confident most of the time
- others looking for your input
- others wanting access to you and willing to wait for you
- good physical health

Signs of Low Rank

- feeling uncomfortable or afraid
- getting interrupted
- others not waiting for you—you wait for them
- you feel you cannot say no to the requests of others
- lacking confidence and not feeling important
- poor physical health

60

Rank Can Be Like a Numbing Drug

One of the essential troubles with rank is the oxymoronic characteristic it tends to have: the more rank you have, the less aware you tend to be of the impact of it on others. When we get some rank, we feel elated, powerful and/or altered in our consciousness. This is especially true if we have felt low-ranked much of our life. Rank is like a drug (Mindell, *Sitting in the Fire*, p. 49).

When I was in the construction supply world, I noticed that when other salesmen became the top producer, they were elated. It was almost like they were a bit drunk. They became the center of attention. They loved the limelight. Sometimes they got loud, almost like a gorilla beating his chest. Their ego got inflated, and others got momentarily forgotten. I noticed these things in others, and eventually also in myself.

An experience of high rank can partially numb us so that our ability to feel and relate to others is limited. When we are out of touch with our own feelings, we are likely to ignore our own emotions and the needs of others. This, coupled with the incessant drive for productivity inherent in the construction world, may lead to a lack of basic empathy. The inability to express empathy for others, and ourselves, is a significant detriment to our capacity to build trusting relationships. And trusting relationships are required for optimal safety accountability.

The ability to practice empathetic leadership, is what is needed to build trust. According to Zach Knoop, General Manager - Safety Services at Caterpillar Inc., empathetic leadership *"... is demonstrated through both words and deeds that you care about those you lead, the customers you serve, and the communities you are part of. But it is more than just care; it is about fostering a diverse and inclusive workplace, one where people feel free to show up and speak up authentically, without fear of being silenced." (from an article in the digital Asphalt Pavement Magazine Jan/Feb 2021 issue, written by Valerie Echter).* This sort of empathy implies a positive use of your rank. Those who misuse rank tend to exclude others and may unintentionally create cultures where people do not feel free to speak up.

Therefore, the way we manage our rank matters. We can have high rank and still pay attention to the needs and feelings of others. Doing so will contribute to the safety and bottom-line interests of the organization.

Rank Can Be a Force for Good and a Contribution to Safety

High rank does not need to function like a drug in our bloodstream. Rank can be used with awareness and sensitivity, becoming a source of positive power. *"Rank is not inherently bad, and abuse of rank is not inevitable. When you are aware of your rank you can use it to your own benefit and the benefit of others as well"* (Mindell, *Sitting in the Fire*, p. 53). Here is a fine example, which happened some years ago in Minnesota to a friend of mine.

The Leak in the Boardroom: A True Story

Ted (not his real name) is the head of business development for a company that helps people keep water and other unwanted things out of their buildings. He is an important guy, and he knows just about everyone in the building business. He is a person with high social and positional rank.

He told me this story some years ago. It is about a skillful use of rank and a powerful example of accountability. One day there was a problem at the global headquarters of a Fortune 500 company in Minnesota at which he was doing some roof repair. Let's call it ABC Corporation. There was a leak in the boardroom used by the internationally known CEO, and they had an important meeting scheduled there with the board of directors. The CEO asked what company was responsible for fixing the roof. They told him the name of that company, and he asked who the key person was at that company. At 7:15 a.m. on Monday Ted's assistant said, *"Ted, you have a call on line 1. It's ABC Corporation. I think they have a problem."* Ted panicked for a moment, took a deep breath, stood up and in his most alert voice said into the phone, *"This is Ted. May I help you?"* It was his secretary: *"Yes, Mr. CEO would like to speak with you. There seems to be a leak in the boardroom."*

"Ted, this is Mr. CEO. You are responsible for fixing leaks in our roof, right?" Ted pretended to be calm. *"Right."* *"What is going on here, Ted? I have a leak in my boardroom, right on the long wooden table where we meet, and I have a board meeting today. Can you solve that right away?"* Ted said, *"I'll get right on it, Mr. CEO."*

Ted called his foreman on the job and found out they had more than one leak. He quickly called Mr. CEO and gave him the news, directly. *"Yes, sir, I am sorry to report that you actually have four leaks in your building now. In addition to the one in the board meeting room, you have two in your 'clean rooms' and one in your shipping warehouse. The boardroom is the fourth."*

There was a pause. Then Mr. CEO said, *"Is there any way you can move the boardroom repair farther down the list?"* Ted said, *"Excuse me, sir? You you're your board room moved further down the list?"* *"Yes. If we have leaks in the surgically clean rooms, we can't build our products. If we have leaks in the warehouse, we can't ship them, and we then have a real problem: we can't be profitable.*

I want my board of directors to sit in the boardroom with a garbage can on the table to catch the water, and I want to say that this company is far more important than I am."

Ted was shocked and said, *"Yes, sir. Not a problem, Mr. CEO. We will get right on it."* All the leaks were eventually fixed, with the boardroom being last. The board met that day, with a garbage can on the boardroom table. Ted was astounded at the humility and maturity of this CEO. Given his high rank, he could have asked for whatever he wanted and gotten it. He could have asked for the boardroom to be repaired first, as a way of asserting his importance. But he did not. His ego did not trump taking care of the right things first. This is a leader who responded to a situation in a mature and inspiring way for the common good of the business and its employees.

This is an example of a perfect use of personal accountability and power. The company continues to be one of the best and most profitable in Minnesota, because of leaders like this CEO who use their rank skillfully for the common good.

The ability to self-modulate one's positional power is a rare skill, especially among men at his level. This kind of selfless leadership is rare everywhere and even more scarce in construction, where unbridled ego-power still holds the day in many organizations. Rank awareness, well used in a challenging situation or interpersonal conflict, can be like a life-saving dose of epinephrine given to a child having a lethal asthma attack. It creates space for others to breathe and to interact in more respectful ways. It inspires the creation of trusting relationships.

It *is possible* for leaders to become aware of how they are using their rank and power and to grow in their capacity to use it in ways that will improve their professional and personal lives.

How would you compare yourself or your current leaders to Mr. CEO in this true story? How is rank being used by your leaders right now? And how is their behavior impacting your work culture and your injuries? Are your owners, C-level leaders, managers and supervisors using their rank with selfless awareness and consistent skill? Have they had the chance to reflect on their leadership style and begun to see and work on their blind spots?

Rank, unrecognized and misused creates dangerous situations on jobsites every day. How many serious injuries and deaths happened in part or completely because of rank misuse? Rank can numb us like a drug, or with the right support, wake us up to our full potential. Make sure all your leaders understand this concept and then get the training and coaching they need to use their rank to influence others as skillfully as possible.

CHAPTER EIGHT

What Construction Companies Can Learn from Airplane Crashes

Now that you have a broader understanding of rank, I want to share some insights from some studies of culture and airplane crashes. You will see how power and rank, unrecognized and poorly used, contributes to catastrophic accidents that mirror what happens in your industry. When teamwork and communication are compromised, safety accountability suffers, and injuries are more likely.

Power has been defined in many ways. Dr. Julie Diamond has written an amazing book called *Power: A User's Guide*. In it she provides some useful definitions of power. Max Weber, the German sociologist defined power as *"the ability to assert one's will over others."* (*Power: A User's Guide, p. 2*) Diamond herself defines power as *"our capacity to impact and influence our environment."* (*Power: A Users Guide*, p. 3) There are times when we need to assert our will over others, but nowadays that style Max Weber was talking about is seen as a last resort. It is more desirable now to influence more by our example and less by the force that lies in our title.

Our capacity to impact and influence our environment is related to the social and contextual rank we have in a given context. And that rank, has become more complex, as the winds of social change are blowing the traditional structures of power around like a fragile tumbleweed, in a manner we have not seen in a long time.

Nevertheless, rank and power still play a huge role in how communication happens and with respect to safety accountability.

Being accountable means being able to take full responsibility for your words and actions. This involves speaking up and being in communication with others, even others who may have higher positional rank than you. In cultures defined by a "command and control" style, especially those with a preponderance of men (such as construction, the military, etc.), it is vital to understand the subtle and not-so-subtle social rules of communicating with those of higher rank.

As we mentioned in chapter four, the general rule for those of lower rank is this: You do not interrupt, speak up to or otherwise bother a person of higher rank. If you have seniority, and high rank because you are the boss, or the superintendent you can more easily speak up to others. You are more likely to influence your environment. That is power. You may not feel powerful, it may feel like a battle to get others to agree that your idea is so good. But you have capacity to influence by virtue of your rank.

Speaking up, especially at a jobsite when something dangerous is happening, is an essential part of safety. If you have top rank you may tell everyone *"Speak up guys!"* and expect that they will. What could keep anyone from speaking up? Part of the reason they may not speak up is related to rank. Until you understand rank and power, and how it works in male-oriented culture, you will not fully grasp what will be required to create a work culture where everyone feels truly free to speak up and listen up. You will know you have a gold-medal safety accountability culture when your lower ranked workers speak up regularly and your higher ranked workers stop, listen and respond every time someone of lower ranks respectfully speaks up.

I recently conducted a three-day safety audit at a company with a fabulous MOD rate (.53) and a strong safety culture. And yet, they have room for growth. They told me that recently they had an injury. A higher ranked worker (a pipelayer) was climbing down an 18' deep manhole when a lower ranked worker (a laborer), did speak up, to a pipelayer. Kudos to that company for creating that kind of culture where a lower ranked person attempted to intervene with a higher ranked worker. Unfortunately, in this case the higher ranked person did not listen to the laborer and did not tie off. He fell down the manhole and broke his ankle. An injury that could have been prevented had he been trained to counteract the typical dynamics of rank.

Having high rank is one factor in safety accountability; how you *use* your rank is what will differentiate you and raise your capacity to influence in the direction of the common good. You could have high rank and have relatively little power if you do not use your rank skillfully.

On the other hand, someone of relatively low positional rank in an organization, such as a laborer or a driver, can sometimes assert their power and get what they want if they have strong psychological rank coupled with a high level of skill.

Those of higher rank tend to be less aware of relational dynamics, and they have more license to do what they want. When someone has high rank, they tend to be:

- not very aware of the feelings and needs of others.

- not very aware of their own impact on others.

- the ones giving feedback and directing others.

- not particularly open to the feedback of those beneath them in rank, especially in high-risk situations.

All these tendencies can add up to cultural communication patterns that magnify risk. A perfect example of risk magnified by rank can be found in Malcolm Gladwell's book, *Outliers*, in his chapter titled, *"An Ethnic Theory of Plane Crashes."* In that chapter he makes two observations about the root causes of the many fatal crashes that happened on Korean airplanes during the 1980s and '90s that are worth repeating here:

1. Traditional Korean cultural patterns of a "command and control" style of social communication contributed to the crashes.

2. Airplane crashes happen not for one reason, but because of at least seven mistakes made by pilots, and involving errors of teamwork and communication.

Command and Control

It is said that Korean culture has two main features germane to this topic: a deep reverence for seniority or age, and an authoritarian style of leadership. It is believed by some writers that those two features, and the way those attributes played out in the cockpit, contributed to the Korean Airlines crashes.

Between 1970 and 1999 so many Korean Airlines airplanes crashed that many were worried that the airlines would go out of business. Sixteen crashes and over 700 people were killed. The situation warranted many studies and eventually an overhaul of their cockpit culture. After an extensive and successful investment in culture change, they went many years with no crashes and were recognized as one of the safest airline companies in the world. They truly transformed themselves. Before the culture change, the lead pilot had absolute authority. The lower-ranked co-pilot would never speak up or offer feedback to him. With the cockpit culture change, they established radically different and egalitarian practices of communication, whereby anyone in the cockpit could offer feedback and input to anyone else, without retribution or animosity. They leveled the playing field of rank and power.

Gladwell has written that airplanes tend to be safer when a less experienced pilot is flying while supervised by a more experienced one, one with higher positional rank. When the reverse is true, he writes, a junior officer is less likely to speak up about potential mistakes or problems to a more senior officer.

The Koreans, to their great credit, learned to override their natural cultural norms to make things safer. This is an amazing example of powerful systemic change, motivated by business interests, leading to fewer injuries and incidents.

Seven Mistakes = One Crash

Gladwell also notes that there are at least seven consecutive human errors that result in a crash. I will repeat a few of them. You can find these on p. 184 of his book *Outliers*:

"In a typical crash the weather is poor—not terrible, but bad enough that the pilot feels a little bit more stressed than usual. In an overwhelming number of crashes, the plane is behind schedule, so the pilots are hurrying."

Sleep is also a factor: "In 52 percent of crashes, the pilot at the time of the accident has been awake for twelve hours or more, meaning that he is tired and not thinking sharply."

And how often the pilots have worked together matters too: "Forty-four percent of the time, the two pilots have never flown together before, so they're not comfortable with each other."

He states that the errors start off relatively small and keep multiplying. Gladwell says it is the combination of the mistakes that leads to disaster. And they are rarely problems of knowledge or flying skill. *"The kinds of errors that cause plane crashes are invariably errors of teamwork and communication."* (p. 184) That comment is potentially so valuable to you, that I am going to repeat it so that you don't miss it:

"The kinds of errors that cause plane crashes are invariably errors of teamwork and communication."

These same kinds of errors are what cause deaths, maiming and injuries in your world.

Not everyone agrees completely with Gladwell's analysis. Some have critiqued it, and others have tested it. IB Psychology used a 1993 study to show that Gladwell's work has merit; you can read about it in an article by Travis Dixon, titled "Power Distance and Plane Crashes: The Gladwell Hypothesis" (*IB Psychology*, May 6, 2020). The article refers to the work of Dutch social psychologist

Geert Hofstede as proof that Gladwell is onto something true. Hofstede developed his original model with extensive data from a worldwide survey of employee values by IBM between 1967 and 1973. It was later updated. Power distance is one of five cultural dimensions Hofstede developed to measure how a culture views power relationships between people. Cultures demonstrating a high power distance index (PDI) view power as distributed unevenly, according to a hierarchy of authority. And in those cultures, people are less *likely to speak up* to someone in authority. People from cultures with a low PDI, view power as distributed more evenly and will be *more likely to speak up*. The index runs from 1 to 104. Malaysia received the highest ranking at 104. Guatemala came in second with a PDI of 95, and Mexico scored an 81. . For more detail on Hofstede's work see *www. clearlycultural.com*.

That means that the average person from Malaysia, Guatemala and Mexico will be considerably deferential to someone in authority. They will be unlikely to speak up, even if you tell them to. Hofstede rated the USA at a PDI of 40. The more homogenous the culture, the more the score should hold true of most people from that country. The more heterogeneous the culture, the less credence there may be in that score. This fact should make us question the USA score, because of our extensive cultural diversity. The lowest score of the 66 countries he studied was Austria, with an 11.

If you have people from Malaysia or Guatemala or Mexico, all things being equal, they will be much like the Korean co-pilots before the culture change—not likely to speak up even in the interest of safety. You will want to get some Austrians in your cockpits—or on your jobsites, if speaking up is a problem for your field workers or foremen.

The research described in that *IB Psychology* article demonstrated that when pilots with less rank don't have the confidence to contradict or challenge their superiors, *"it increases the chances of an accident."*

What do airplane crashes, and the power distance index have to do with your construction world? A lot. The lessons learned from Gladwell and Hofstede have direct application to your world. They point out that rank, power and culture matter when it comes to people speaking up in the interest of safety, and that accidents happen not for one reason, but because of many factors that come together at the same moment, including lack of sleep, feeling rushed, weather and communication. And maybe even more importantly, rank and power.

Those of us who have been in and around construction culture for a long time, or any place where the rules of hierarchy are strictly enforced know that speaking up is more difficult in these environments.

While good general knowledge of construction work is useful, the skill level of your workers is not primarily what causes or prevents injuries. Good communication is vital for injury prevention. Just as in plane crashes, the quality of teamwork and communication is very important. And the way in which rank and power are used has a huge influence on the quality of your teamwork and the effectiveness of your communication.

Here is the good news: with the right approach, and training, you can get people to override their cultural and personal tendencies and communicate differently, just like they did in the Korea industry decades ago. You can also coach workers into taking greater personal responsibility for their words and actions. It will not be easy. It will take a small revolution, and a focused effort over a length of time, probably years. But it will be well-worth it. And it will make you a transformational leader.

No One Spoke Up

I had been calling on a safety leader friend at a large company in the Midwest for some years, back when I was doing demo saw safety. For a few years he said they were fine and did not need any demo saw safety. Then in less than a month he had two injuries, one of them was very serious.

The regular sawman was gone that day on vacation. One of possibly seven mistake-conditions. It was a 72" pipe, and since he didn't take time to build some scaffolding or find another safe way to cut, he had the saw above his shoulders. He also did not have the pipe properly supported. So, at least three things were going wrong that we know of.

These saws are 25-30 pounds and have incredible torque. Most workers on a jobsite know that they should not operate such machinery above their shoulders, because they do not have enough leverage to manage the tool. At some point, as he was getting close to finishing the job the concrete shifted, pinched the blade and there was a violent kickback. The saw pinwheeled up in the air and he held on with one hand. The saw came down with the blade still spinning and cut through his boot, nearly severing his foot. A very painful and expensive injury.

That type of incident, a demo saw "pushback," happens more often than you think. It is commonly and mistakenly known as kickback—as only saws with cutting teeth that have positive rake angle can kickback. It happens because of operator error and causes about 10-15 deaths per year, according to Rick Norland, owner of Construction Solutions, LLC. Rick is one of the people, providing expert testimony for Stihl USA when there is a death or a legal case, because of his deep knowledge of cutting with demo saws.

There were at least 7 people on that jobsite, at the time, any one of whom could have spoken up and prevented an injury. No one spoke up. I have empathy with those on the jobsite, because I know it takes real courage to interrupt, especially someone with the high rank of a skilled heavy machine operator.

How might that interruption have sounded had that company been though my complete safety accountability program?

Craftworker to foreman: "Time out! Hey, time out there.!!" (getting in his field of vision, waving his hand)

Foreman: "What?" (he can't hear, it is too loud)

Craftworker: "Time out!!!! Can you please stop for a minute?"

Foreman: (foreman stops, looks irritated)

Craftworker: "Excuse me sir, I know I am well under you by title and experience, but I do know that it isn't safe to run a tool like that."

Foreman: "Hey buddy, I've been doing this 10X longer than you. Mind your own business."

Craftworker: "I know you are truly seasoned. And I just did my OSHA 10 and learned that you should never have a demo saw above your shoulders like that. And I like you as a boss and would not want to see you injured."

Foreman: "Oh really now? That's peachy." (still intending to finish the work)

Craftworker: "Hey, would your kids want you doing that?" (knowing he has 3 small kids). I'll bet we can find a safer way to do this."

Foreman: "Well…"

Craftworker: "You know more than I do. You are the boss. And I'll bet you know how to get a scaffolding up on this, or find a safer way to do it that is still efficient"

Foreman: (thinking)

Craftworker: I can help, I just finished up cutting that concrete slab

Foreman: "Ok, you are right…"

Craftworker: "Thanks for listening, what do we need?"

74

We are not trained to interrupt, especially if we have lower rank. And we are not trained to handle the resistance that is likely to come when one worker interrupts another. It does not matter if we are from Mexico or the USA or Malaysia. Especially in construction, maybe not at your company, but many contractors tend to let people do whatever they want, even if they are taking a shortcut, or doing something risky. What they need is a skillful, respectful and powerful interruption. They need someone brave, like you, to intervene. They need someone to say or do something to get them to stop and reconsider what they are doing.

Having high rank can make it hard for us to be accountable to others, because of the inherent nature of rank. It tends to make us less aware of the experiences, needs and feelings of others. The key to becoming accountable lies in becoming aware of the rank-power we possess. We do not need to be a Korean pilot or from a high PDI country to need some support communicating with others. We can wake up to the rank and power we do have to influence the decisions and behavior of others. The advantages we have, by virtue of our title, personality, economic wealth, physical health or our social standing among others—when well-used— can make a real difference in creating a strong culture of safety accountability.

If your company is at all like Korean Airlines was, where lower ranked workers do not speak up to higher ranked workers, then you are ripe for some training and coaching in rank awareness and effective use of rank. Doing so might just prevent an expensive series of accidents and crashes.

CHAPTER NINE

Put on Your Big Boy Pants!

I was at an annual gathering at a construction company some years ago, and the owner said something I'll never forget. He said:

"We had too many injuries last year, guys. Accidents happen when we are distracted. Someone yells and another guy gets pissed off. It's a problem. Put on your big boy pants, guys! Be a good communicator. Stay focused on the job."

This was one of the most emotionally intelligent and courageous things I've ever heard a leader at a construction company say to their workers. He was asking them to take personal responsibility for their actions and words. He was passionate because they had some accidents that happened in the context of workers being upset with each other. He was also empathetic in his tone; he truly cares about his workers. Accidents happen when we are distracted. True, but why? And what can we do about it?

You know about the "fight, flight or freeze" part of your brain. It is also called the "reptilian brain." It is meant to protect us when we are threatened. If a 10-point buck comes from nowhere, charging you, like one did to a guy I know who was bow hunting in Nebraska, you need to react quickly. That is when you need a rush of adrenaline to save your own life. The aggressive buck was 10 feet away, and the hunter quickly pulled back his bow. Perfect shot. The charging animal dropped dead in its tracks, just a few feet away. The hunter's quickness and accuracy were no doubt fueled by the immediate rush of adrenaline initiated by his reptilian brain. A perfect example of the reptilian brain in action. Nicely done, Jack.

The reptilian part of your brain is very powerful and hyperreactive. It may easily boss you around. It is passionate about self-protection and ultimately survival. It tends to overestimate the seriousness of a threat. Someone may be trying to help you avoid injury, by shouting in your direction, but your brain interprets their loud yelling as a threat. It may not even be close to a life-threatening moment, like a large buck charging you at close range, but your brain doesn't know that. Whenever you feel a threat, your amygdala rapidly sends out cortisol and adrenaline, preparing your body to flee or fight to the death if necessary.

Flight or fight seem to be the favorite choices of this part of our brain. Freezing is also an option, but not a very attractive one. Fleeing seems like a coward's choice and not one you want to make in a tough-guy culture. Punching that fellow who is an absolute jerk seems like a good idea when your amygdala is in the driver's seat, but is it in your best interest?

The most accountable leaders want all their workers to have more control over their actions. The owner of the company I was visiting that day suggested three things:

#1 "Put on your big boy pants."

This is great advice because we all tend to act like young children when we get triggered. He suggests that we act like adults, even when we are having strong emotions and feeling threatened by another person.

What does *"put on your big boy pants"* mean? It means that you do what adults would do: manage your emotions, do the responsible thing. It means that if that regressed, childlike side of yourself takes the wheel, the more mature side needs to take the wheel back. This is one way to avoid a crash.

I am aware that this sort of taking back the wheel is incredibly challenging for all of us. Even those of us who have had a lot of training in just how to do that still find it hard to do. But it is possible, and necessary if you want a trophy-sized level of safety accountability.

#2 "Be a good communicator."

This means that you will talk with others and say the right things. You will speak words that are helpful, respectful and clear. And you will have a tone of voice and body language that get the results you want. If the person truly is doing something that requires raising your voice, do that. And then, since a loud voice usually triggers a reaction, go up to them later and check in. Do this as soon as it is safe to do so. Reaffirm that they are a good worker—if they are—and that you want them around as long as possible.

#3 "Stay focused on the job."

Staying focused can be difficult after you get emotionally triggered. You may be quietly fuming or unable to think. Or if you are honest and reflective, you might realize that you feel anxious or even hurt. You might have strong feelings, but you are not even sure what they are. You pretend you are fine. But there is no doubt you are *distracted*. You are not able to do your job as safely as when you are not triggered. This has happened to me. Years ago, I once spent nearly two hours being distracted from my job. I was so upset at some other workers, because of a racial incident that happened in Minneapolis and their response to it, that I simply could not concentrate, and I was very unproductive. Fortunately, I was indoors that entire time, not on a huge piece of machinery, and no one was injured because of my being distracted.

When you are not focused on your work, you are ineffective at best. When you are doing construction with heavy equipment all around you, you are at higher risk of injury. And equally importantly, you are of no help to your fellow workers.

This is largely due to your distracted brain. So perhaps you forget to check your mirrors while driving, and you cause an accident. Or you move too quickly and tear into a gas line with the excavator. Maybe you forget to properly support the material you are cutting with a demo saw. The blade pinches and the saw kicks back violently. You suffer a serious laceration to your throat.

Injuries and deaths happen regularly on jobsites all over America, partly because of workers with distracted brains. And currently, with the pandemic, the economic downturn and the racial unrest, most of us are experiencing more stress. G. Brent Darnell, one of the foremost experts on emotional intelligence in the architecture, engineering and construction (AEC) industry, suggests that when you are stressed, *"your body is in a low-level fight/flight state. It is being flooded with adrenaline and cortisol. . . .*

Breathing becomes shallow, which reduces oxygen to your brain, your blood flow goes to the extremities, and your thinking brain actually shuts down." (Darnell, *The People-Profit Connection*, p. 55).

The prefrontal cortex, where we do our best logical thinking, is less active when we are triggered. When the reptile part of the brain lights up, the thinking part shuts off. That is when the diapers can easily come on. You must turn off the reptile part and turn on the thinking part of your brain in order to be a safe, effective and accountable leader. The good news is that you can do this fairly quickly. In the next chapter we will outline some practical ideas on how to train your reptilian brain, how to keep the lights on in your rational brain.

CHAPTER TEN

How to Train Your Reptilian Brain

"You must teach your workers stress reduction techniques such as meditation, mindfulness, and deep breathing." —G. Brent Darnell, *The People-Profit Connection*

Are you a little disturbed by the idea that you *"must teach"* your people *"meditation, mindfulness, and deep breathing?"* Are you wondering, just how touchy feely we are going to get? Don't worry. This chapter is not about touchy or feely and we are not asking you to become a Buddhist monk. Managing your reptilian brain is about control. If you want your people to have more power over their hormonally charged responses to stress and threats, then yes, you must offer them techniques that restore control. It is about teaching them ways to manage their natural responses so that they can say and do the right thing, especially in high stakes situations.

It is possible to train your brain to work differently than it does by its own instincts. You can gain greater control over your behavior, by practicing certain tried and true techniques. They will allow you to respond calmly and logically during high-intensity situations that happen regularly in construction.

Brent Darnell, has been training construction workers in these very techniques for decades. He is doing some of the most cutting-edge work with behavior control and emotional intelligence in the construction world. He understands the flight-flight-flee stress response as well as anyone I know. And he understands that the training required to prevent your reptile brain from taking over is holistic—it is grounded in physical well-being, mental health and spiritual maturity.

For some, we need to first address the needs of the body, such as diet, exercise, sleep, etc. Then we can teach them how to manage their natural neurological reactions. We know it is often a good idea to take a break when emotions are running high. Some time and space to cool off will allow for clearer thinking. But you can't always do that, especially in the world of construction. A better solution is to be prepared internally. To develop your brain so that you can stay calm even when others are not.

How do we teach workers, who may have a host of other challenges, to manage their brains and calm themselves down? Here are seven things you can do either right in the moment, or as preparation to maintain control.

1. *Understand* that this is how we are all hard-wired, or more accurately "soft-wired" as John Arden writes. You can read more about his ideas in his book *Rewire Your Brain: Think Your Way to a Better Life*, 2010 by John B. Arden. We all respond to perceived or real threats by an autonomic response that is not easy to control. It is not because we are good or bad. So do not put yourself or others down because of this natural survival instinct.

2. Do your best to *not trigger the survival instincts of others*. As you realize that all brains operate this way, it should make you more aware of the triggers of your co-workers. You can make it less likely that others will go into a fight-flight-freeze pattern by the way you communicate. Even speaking too quickly or loudly can trigger some brains into a survival situation. Knowing the emotional hot buttons of co-workers and not pressing them is very helpful.

3. *Learn your body signals* that indicate your brain thinks you are in the midst of a life-or-death situation. Most men in

construction will not easily admit that they feel threatened. But bodies do not lie, and if we could hook up an fMRI machine to your brain during an intense moment, we could see the lively activity in the limbic region, where the amygdala resides. And most likely we would see almost no electrical energy in the prefrontal cortex, the rational thinking area. If you can notice the smallest little signals that you feel threatened, it can be enough to wake you up and allow you to modulate your ability to control your feelings, thoughts and actions. For me, it is tension in my gut and in my neck. I also feel a racing sensation in my mind and an urgency to act. What are your signals?

4. *Slow down the automatic reaction to fight, flee or freeze.* As a child you may have heard some advice about what to do when you are upset: *"If you are angry or scared count to 10."* That was good advice, because that is about how quickly we can restore the thinking part of our brain. And it works whether we are angry, scared or just irritated. Science says it takes as little as six seconds to get the amygdala to quiet down and the prefrontal cortex (the rational-thinking part of the brain) to fully engage and function. This is backed by a Harvard Business Review article called, *Just 6 Seconds of Mindfulness Can Make You More Effective* by Chade-Meng Tan, December 30, 2015.

5. *Counting along with breathing* is even more effective for slowing things down. This was demonstrated by Dr. Andrew Weil who decades ago created a breathing technique, as a de-stressor and to slow down the physiological response to a threat. He calls it the 4-7-8 method. It very simple and one of the most effective things you can do to control your mind and calm your nervous system. You can do it now. Breathe in through your nostrils for four seconds. Hold your breath, while relaxing your shoulders, for seven seconds. Then breathe out, through pursed lips, for eight seconds. Do this for four cycles, twice a day for a month, and then you can raise the number of cycles. Weil recommends you do it for no more than eight cycles. It can

also be used for sleep, anxiety and to reduce cravings. As the Zen Buddhist monk *Thích Nhất Hạnh* puts it, *"Feelings come and go like clouds in a windy sky. Conscious breathing is my anchor."*

6. ***Reduce the loss of emotional control by training yourself, to not react strongly***, but rather to keep control of your thinking function. This is the long game—what you do on the golf tee, not when you are near the green. There are many things you can do to reduce your reactivity to external stimuli, whether it is another person yelling, or a highly stressful situation. I will quickly outline three of them: meditation, emotional intelligence training and hot button reduction.

   A. Meditation: One of the most effective means to improve your mental, spiritual and emotional health is meditation. It is also one of the main ways you can gain more control over your automatic responses. There have been many brain studies, since the invention of the functional MRI machine in the 1990s. That machine allows researchers to see what is happening in the brain in real time. Meditation enables you to have more control over your naturally reactive neurological tendencies.

   And of all people studied, who do you think has the most control over their autonomic reactions to external stimuli? Seasoned Buddhist monks. People who have spent thousands of hours meditating in silence. They have changed the workings of their brains via mediation. (See "Meditation affects brain networks differently in long-term meditators and novices", University of Wisconsin-Madison, NEWS. July 23, 2018 By Marianne Spoon.) I know that most of your workers are probably not Buddhist monks, let alone seasoned ones. But all of us are capable of learning mindfulness mediation or take time for silent prayer. It has also been shown that a small amount of mediation can lead to positive brain capacity.

(See "Are We Morally Obligated to Meditate?" by Sigal Samuel, June 2020, Vox Media.)

Perhaps you already pray or find time for devotions. Silent meditation, for 10-20 minutes a day can be very effective, not only for your own spiritual life but also for your ability to deal with stress and difficult co-workers. I suggest you take time daily for meditation. You may want to get some assistance with this, because sitting in silence for 20 minutes is harder than you think. This kind of meditation will change the capacity of your brain, over time. It will give you more control over your feelings and reactions.

B. Emotional Intelligence Training   As you increase your emotional intelligence you will reduce the tendency to lose control, in tense situations. It is now almost universally known that high emotional intelligence (EI) is a prerequisite for effective leadership. You can be very technically skilled, and even intellectually brilliant, but if you are not emotionally intelligent, you may not be very effective over the long haul. We will not go into the details of this EI training, as there are many good books on this topic. I will refer to you chapter eighteen, "The Man Box Culture," for one of the best and simplest ideas on how to grow your emotional intelligence.

C. Hot Button Reduction. Have you ever had anyone push one of your hot buttons? Ever worse, in front of a group. Ouch! How did you handle it?

I developed this theory after gaining my Masters in Conflict Facilitation and Organizational Change in 2009, based on some of the ideas of Dr. Arnold Mindell and other teachers I studied with at the Process Work Institute in Oregon. It is simple: your hot buttons shrink as you forgive everyone who ever hurt you. It is becoming common knowledge in the therapeutic world that our triggers of reactivity are almost always directly linked to a significant person injury, either psychological or physical.

The key lies in forgiveness. According to Fred Kiel, in *Return on Character*, Forgiveness is *"Letting go of one's mistakes—and those of others; focusing on what's right versus what's wrong."* (p. 64) When we have let go of their mistake or ours, done by that person or organization who hurt us, or the situation itself, or maybe even God, then our hot button shrinks and becomes warm. Eventually it is at room temperature and we can barely remember why we were so upset before. It is no longer hot. So, they can push that button, but we will not react. That is how we know we've healed something painful in our past.

7. ***Change the culture at your company.*** This final idea is the most revolutionary because it will involve everyone. It is the heroic and inspiring work of culture change. You may think *"We are doing fine Tom, we do not need to change our culture, we like our culture."* Or *"We are doing better than most other contractors in our town. This isn't for us."* Perhaps. But how would you rate the trust level and average emotional maturity of everyone in your company? Are all your leaders open to receiving feedback from others, especially in moments of heightened intensity? Would they stop to listen to a lower ranked person? Changing your culture is the most challenging of these suggestions but it can be done. It may take some years to achieve the changes you want, but it is possible and just might be the most exciting "project" you ever embarked upon.

Doing even some of the seven ideas above will begin to help your people re-train the reptilian part of their brain. These will help improve your chances of having workers who can stay calm and speak up in the interest of safety. I now want to share a true story of a difficult situation I had with a neighbor many years ago that involved an opportunity to calm myself in the heat of the moment.

The Story of the Barking Dog

I have done the "count to six" method of brain control a few times in my life, even when being yelled at. It is not easy to remember to do it, but if you can, I assure you it really works!

My wife and I were living in South Minneapolis and the new neighbor's dog barked a lot. He was a half-crazy dog who once scaled the cyclone fence he was behind and nearly killed our cat. His nightly barking was starting to drive us crazy. One summer night, at 11:30 p.m., my wife said, *"Honey, you've got to shut that f—ing dog up!"* So, I did the only thing a modern, urban knight would do, I picked up my cellphone and called the man of the house. I left a voicemail, something like this: *"Hi there Dave, it is your neighbor Tom. Your dog is barking, and we can't sleep. I wonder if we can solve that…"*

The next day I saw my neighbor up on a ladder, about 15 feet in the air. I started talking to him: *"I hope you got my voicemail, I—"* But he interrupted me, yelling loudly, *"If you can't take a little barking, why don't you move to the f—ing country!"* I was shocked. My peripheral vision started to narrow. I said, *"Well, maybe we **should** move to the country… but until we do… we have a problem."*

He escalated, raising his voice even louder and gesturing in my direction. My training kicked in. I paused and started to count to six. When I hit six, it was like a switch flipped. I could think clearly and saw a bigger picture. I realized that he was 15 feet in the air, getting more animated and angrier. I imagined him falling off the ladder, into my yard and suing me. This was not the way I wanted this story to end.

So, instead I said, *"Dave, time out, I see you are on a ladder, so I want to stop talking now, but would like to resume the conversation later."*

For more than a week he did not make eye contact with me.

Eventually, I reflected on my part in the drama. I wrote a sincere apology. This was not easy to do.

I apologized for calling him at 11:30 p.m., which was too late, and then for trying to have a serious conversation while he was 15 feet up on a ladder, which was unsafe and ineffective. I said it would not happen again.

A few days later, he invited me over for a beer, which is a guy's way of saying *"I accept your apology."* He never apologized, and I didn't expect him to. He was not aware of his own behavior, and I didn't think it would be helpful for me to point it out.

And as for the barking dog, it all ended sadly for them. His dog attacked the neighbor's dog and had to be put to sleep. This in turn helped our sleep. Things have a way of eventually working out.

Yes, we can control our reptilian natural impulses with the right training, attention and discipline. Your amygdala wants to protect you, but it sometimes does the opposite and triggers an overreaction that endangers you. Your job is to keep the lights on in your pre-frontal cortex. To counterbalance the immediate flow of cortisol and adrenaline that have already been released, preparing you to fight or flee. Now you have some new tools to keep calm. Don't let them stay in your toolbox. Take them out and use them regularly. Practice them with others. These will enable you to stay in control, be calm, and speak up. Maybe you will not turn Buddhist, but you just might become a safety accountability ninja.

CHAPTER ELEVEN

Build Trust by Admitting Mistakes and Cleaning Up Messes

Trust is not automatic. It is earned over time and lost easily.

C leaning up your people-messes and admitting your mistakes are two ways to build trust. Cleaning up your messes is different from admitting your mistakes. Admitting a mistake is saying, *"I put the oil on the edge of the work bench. My mistake."* Cleaning it up is getting shop rags and paint thinner to properly clean it off the floor, and then taking care of the relationships you have with all of those impacted by your mistake. How you clean up your "messes" impacts the quality of trust between you and others. Just remember the physical mess is only part of the equation. And trust is an essential part of safety accountability.

Saying *"Yes, I put it there, but Billy knocked it off when he ran the drill press and the work bench vibrated"* is not helpful.

"I'm sorry I did that." "It was my mistake." "I will clean it up now." *"It happened because I was in a hurry."* Those are all excellent things you could say at the moment it happened, if you are aware and willing.

You want to take full ownership of the mistake. "Extreme ownership", as Jocko Willink and Leif Babin call it in their book by that same name. See chapter eighteen "Personal Integrity and Trust" for a thorough explanation of what they mean by "extreme" and "ownership." Basically, it means taking fully responsibility; being 100% accountable for what you did or did not do. In this case, cleaning up both the physical "mess" and the relationship "mess."

Later, after cleaning it up, you could show awareness and empathy by saying something like this, *"Hey do you have a minute to talk about that spill I caused?"* They say, *"Sure, ok." "I'll bet that my putting that gallon of dirty oil right on the edge of the work bench, so it later fell off and spilled everywhere, really put a dent in your day. You couldn't work in that area until it was cleaned up later."* And they might reply, *"Yep, that's true." "Which caused you to get less done."* They say something like *"Yes, right on, Einstein."* You just eat the crow and put a little salsa on it and then get him a six-pack of his favorite beer for the weekend.

Admitting your mistake is the first part, and then cleaning it up is the second part. If you only admit the mistake and do not clean it up, you jeopardize the trust between you.

What does "cleaning up" involve when it comes to people?

Thinking about the impact on them. This usually means guessing about the impact, since it is a rare person who will give you any details.

"When I called you a 'dumb ass' yesterday in front of the whole crew, that was not respectful. I'm sorry I did that. I'll bet you were pissed off at me for a while." "Yeah, I was." "I am not sure what the impact was on you, or how to make it up to you, but I promise it won't happen

again." And then buy the guy a big bag of his favorite beef jerky to give him before his hunting trip. That should help rebuild the relationship and restore the trust between you.

Here is another example in which I made a mess that needed some clean up. It was August 2008, and I was selling supplies in a family business owned by one of my brothers. We all were feeling extra pressure as the economic picture continued to worsen locally and nationally. We were developing a new process for shredding confidential papers. We were asked to put our papers into a big blue bin in the warehouse, with a tiny slot for an opening to ensure privacy. Then a shredding company would come to unlock and dump the blue bins. I took my big pile of papers to the bin one day and realized, that because of the small slot, it would take more time than I thought it would. I had a huge box. So, I planned to do it my own more efficient way. I would wait until the company came to shred our papers and just hand them my box. I didn't see any problem with that.

Not long after my decision to do it my own way, I saw the woman from the shredding company in the warehouse picking up our two blue bins. As she was leaving the building, I asked her, *"Hey, can you wait a moment while I got my box of paper?"* She looked at me with an expression that said, *"Are you serious?"* and Dave, one of the delivery guys, attempted to interrupt me to help her. He said something to me about not making her wait. I ignored him. Raising my voice and speaking over Dave across the whole warehouse I asked with a little more urgency, *"Hey, can you wait until I get my box, it will take only a half a minute?"* She gave a reluctant affirmative response. She had to wait about half a minute, maybe a bit more.

A few days after the shredding scene in the warehouse Angela, one of the company administrators, walked into my office and said to me, *"Tom Esch is selfish."* I reacted to her angrily, *"What?"* She calmly said, *"That's what I heard. They say you made the shredding lady wait."* I had a real strong inner reaction and in a sharp tone of voice asked: *"Who said that!!?"* She would not give any names. *"Dave?"* I guessed. *"Rodney?"* She would not say. *"I want to speak with them. That is bullshit!!"* I yelled. *"It was like 30 seconds."* She said nothing. I felt hot anger growing inside. *"Tell whoever it is to come and see me, will you?"* She was not willing. Then I said to her, *"Yes, maybe I was selfish that day...."* Then I said, with more than a hint of sarcasm, *"...but I'm probably not the only one around here who is selfish. I don't think I have a monopoly on that one!"* Angela said nothing. I was fuming as she left.

In general, I think of myself as a generous person. At times I think, *"I used to be a priest, that is proof. I was willing to give up marriage and family to serve others."* So, when Angela said to me, point blank, *"Tom Esch is selfish"* it disturbed my self-identity. Her comment was so bothersome that I got triggered and cursed in her presence, something that is not common for me to do.

Waiting can be a big deal in a business setting. Even for 30 seconds. Waiting means time lost, time lost means money lost. I did not know the background to the lady from the shredding company. I learned later that she was in trouble with her boss for taking too much time to collect papers to be shredded. She was on the brink of losing her job. So, Dave, who knew that was attempting to help her out. And I, because of my higher rank than both, ignored their feedback (his comment and her body language) and made her wait. Those with less rank typically wait more than those with more rank. I successfully ignored both of them. Seems subtle but over time these kinds of small errors in rank use add up and cause a lot of irritating messes.

Because of the conversation with Angela and further reflection on my own, I did go back to Dave a few days later and attempted a mess clean up. "I know I didn't treat you right with the situation with the woman who was here to shred our confidential papers. I know you said something, but I didn't even hear it. I was just trying to get my papers shred and you knew something I did not. It would have been good for me to have listened more to what you were trying to say. I want you to know I am working on that and will have more awareness in the future." He said, *"Yeah, I wanted you to know she needed to leave. OK, that would be good."* I felt good about that little talk. He seemed happy that I shared with him my side of it and admitted that I had not treated him right.

I also went back in the warehouse one day to help, as my "personal penance" and worked for about two hours, doing some heavy lifting for them. This was something the sales guys almost never did during that time. The guys in the warehouse seemed to appreciate my help. And I did not make the shredding lady wait again, I decided to put my papers in the tiny slot the way others did. All of this took some extra time, but it was worth it, because it helped me get along better with my workmates.

Going the extra step when cleaning up messes is what people who want to maintain a high level of trust do. Why? Because what you did may have had a bigger impact than you think. We all tend to minimize the damage we do in making mistakes, especially when we are the one with higher rank. We do not fully consider the other person's experience of what happened. We are moving too fast, focused on the next task, not on their thoughts or feelings. So, cleaning up that oil spill is way better than not cleaning it up. But cleaning it up and then buying them something, and showing some empathy, can help them forget the hassle they experienced and can rebuild the trust. They end up thinking *"What a good guy."* Or *"What a thoughtful lady."* instead of *"What a jerk!"*

You never know all the hot buttons of another person, especially a person you do not get along super great with in the first place. They may connect your mistake to another time in their life when the consequences were even higher. If so, you will have some work to do in rebuilding trust with them.

Remember, trust can take years to build and can be destroyed in a moment. So, when you make your next mistake, take personal responsibility, apologize properly, and then do all that is needed to clean it up, physically and relationally. Doing this will make you more accountable and help to create a healthy work culture—emotionally and physically safe.

CHAPTER TWELVE

The Power of a Fake Apology

"If you yell at someone, apologize." —Joe Holtmeier, owner of Holtmeier Construction, Mankato, Minnesota

A fake apology is very powerful. The impact can make a real difference in your relationship with the other person. It may damage it for a long time. A real apology is a good idea after yelling at someone and it is not that easy to do.

It is relatively easy to deliver a fake apology. If you are not sincerely sorry and willing to change your behavior, do not apologize. If you are late to a regular meeting for many times, do not say, *"Sorry, guys, I was busy with another call."* You are not sorry, and no one believes it or expects you to change. A fake apology may sound like a true apology to you, but not to them. The person you are speaking to is the judge. If they feel it is real, it probably is, though it is unlikely they will ever tell you. It takes courage, trust, and a solid sense of self-esteem to properly apologize.

Fake Apology #1: *"I'm sorry you. . ."*

This is the beginning of a fake and ineffective apology. When your apology starts with those three words— *"I'm sorry you . . ."*—you are headed down a dead-end road. It's not going to get you anywhere with the other person. It should sound more like *"I'm sorry I . . ."* Use the first-person singular twice in that first sentence, and you are going to be closer to an effective apology.

Fake Apology #2: *"I'm sorry you felt that way."*

This is one of the most common, and most dangerous, fake apologies. This can seriously set you back with the person you want to apologize to. A fake apology like this calls their feelings into question or even dismisses them entirely. You are not sorry for how they felt. You are sorry for what you did or did not do. It is arrogant and inconsiderate to talk with them like this. Kind of like saying, *"I would not have felt that way, but I see that you did. Sorry that your emotional life is so faulty."*

Fake Apology #3: *"Sorry. I'll try better next time."*

The error here was pointed out brilliantly in Star Wars by Yoda: *"Do, or do not. There is no try."* Just admit what you did, say you will do better next time, and then commit to changing your behavior or attitude. It is that simple.

How to Make a Real Apology

Every relationship has challenges, and things like COVID-19, racial unrest, and economic stress can make things worse. Authentic apologies can help relieve stress and improve accountability. It takes real courage to apologize authentically, especially if there are legal implications. But the benefits are amazing when apologies are skillful and come from the heart!

You may be thinking, construction workers can't talk like this. They use rougher, simpler language. Maybe. And maybe not. Your apology can start with something like, *"I am sorry that I . . ."* Then it continues: *"because I imagine that it had this impact on you . . so I apologize, because . . ."* It does not hurt to say the apology twice, since many people are not used to hearing an authentic one. And to put the icing on the cake, say: *""Here is what I will do to make up for it . . .and here is what I plan to do going forward."* Wow!

When you make the real apology, your voice and body language must indicate true sorrow, actual regret. Study all the politicians who have given fake apologies—there are plenty of examples. Watch their body language and notice their tone of voice. Do they seem truly sorry? I can empathize with them, because I too have made many fake apologies. And along the way, I've actually made some real ones as well.

One of my teachers from my seminary training, Fr. Frank Quinlivan once said, *"All the stories are true, and some even happened."* The following is a true story. And it happened.

It happened many years ago, when I was selling construction supplies. I was working for my brother, who was the boss and the owner. It was a good job. We were a good team, and we worked out the "family stuff" with respect and care for each other.

One day I noticed that one of my co-workers was unhappy about something I had done. My first instinct was to ignore him, because it seemed to me that he was just in a mood. However, after some reflection, and considerable help from one of my teachers, I became aware of how I was misusing my rank with him and that I needed to make a real apology. It was my behavior, more than his mood, that was making it easy for him to be upset.

The interaction centered on finding small saw parts in the warehouse. Since these items represented a relatively small part of our sales, finding them was not a priority for me or any of the other sales guys. The way we usually located parts was by asking for help from one of the mechanics in the warehouse, who knew better than we did where the parts were kept. Many of the salesmen did this, even though the mechanic had taken the time to label every single part and put it into a specific, numbered bin and then had created an online schematic so we could find parts ourselves. There were hundreds, maybe thousands, of parts. It had to have been quite a project. Then, during a company meeting, he had asked us all, with real passion in his voice, to "please use the schematics and stop interrupting" him.

The next day a customer called me about replacing a spark plug on one of his tools—a Stihl TS 420 demo saw. I said I'd bring it right over since I was just about to leave for an appointment with him. Since I was in a rush, I asked the mechanic in the warehouse, *"Hey, can you help me find this part?"* He responded, *"Why don't you find the parts yourself?"* I told him I was not good at looking for things and it was easier to just ask him. He did not seem pleased with my reply. He said, *"No, go use the schematics."* I said, *"Plus, I have an appointment across town in 30 minutes; I need it now. Can't you just point out the location?"* He snapped back, *"Go use the schematics."* I said again, *"I don't think I have the time."* Can you guess who won this little battle?

I did. I outranked him. He must have been furious.

About four hours later this co-worker spoke to me in a gruff tone: *"You don't care about finding your own parts; no one does."* He was moving around quickly as he spoke to me, and in his tone of voice I could hear his anger. *"No,"* I said, *"I do care. I want us to work together efficiently."* He said, *"I don't believe it."* I said, *"You are entitled to your beliefs."*

As I walked away, I felt surprised and reflective. I asked myself silently, *"Wow, why is he so upset? And do I really care about what he wants me to do?"* The answers I gave myself sounded like this: *"He has no real reason to be upset; it would have taken him just 30 seconds. What's the big deal? He is wrong. I do care about finding parts using his method. I just haven't had the time to learn it yet. He's just a moody mechanic."* But the interaction bothered me, and I wanted to learn more about what was going on between us.

That evening, I had a meeting with one of my professors. At the time, I was working on a master's degree in conflict resolution, and this was a real live conflict. She read me the riot act on my behavior. I defended. She did not back down. She pointed out that I had pulled rank on this guy. *"How do you know that he wasn't furious that entire four-hour time block, and that he didn't make mistakes fixing saws? And how do you know that he isn't so irritated at the sales staff that he's considering leaving? And why was your need for a part more important than his need to not be interrupted?"*

I said, *"Because I was, at that time, more valuable to the business. I was a salesman earning the revenue that made the company profitable. More revenue than the mechanic. My brother would have wanted me to do this."* (Wow, the unconscious arrogance!) She said, *"And he was one of the mechanics fixing tools; that had to be important."* We had a very intense dialogue. With my professor's help, I got into his shoes and empathized with his perspective. Eventually I saw her point and agreed that I had dismissed his request, had interrupted him while he was working, steam rolled him and owed him an apology.

The guy who knows where the saw parts are has plenty to do. He is fixing tools, managing people and organizing thousands of parts. And the salesmen, including me, had interrupted him probably hundreds of times. We had ignored his request for a long time. There was a history to this situation. As there is in *every* situation.

A few years later my brother (the company owner) said that warehouse mechanic was perhaps the most—not the least—valuable of all the workers. Since his quality repair work and straight-forward manner of communicating pleased most customers. They would then buy other parts while visiting the shop.

What I Did:

So, I went to the mechanic I had steamrolled, and I served myself a big slice of humble pie. I said, *"I am sorry that I ignored your request to use the schematics. That wasn't right. And you said I didn't care about the schematics, and I didn't. And that was wrong. Plus, I interrupted you while you were working, and I pulled rank on you. None of this shows any respect for you. I'm sorry for it. I can imagine that my behavior made it easy for you to feel angry at me. And you were justified, given the history around here and my behavior on many occasions. I pledge to use the schematics to find parts and do my best to not interrupt you."* He was listening intently and had a very big smile on his face by the end. He accepted the apology.

I added, since I knew the new system would be hard for me to get used to, *"There may be a time when I just cannot find the part on the schematics. If that happens, may I come to you to ask for help?"* He agreed. We were nearly friends. And that isn't easy to do with a mechanic.

Apologizing—and taking responsibility for our behavior properly—is related to profitability and to safety. Although it might not have occurred to you previously, a true apology can create safety as it promotes taking responsibility for actions. Responsibility creates accountability, which is like vitamin C for the safety "immune system." The better the communication is between workers—the more skillfully they can identify and isolate potential hazards—the safer everyone is on the job.

How do I know this? I watch the way people treat each other at the places where I lead trainings, and I track the reported injuries in the many organizations where I have worked. Companies with poor communication patterns invariably have more recorded injuries and more near injuries (sometimes mistakenly called "near misses").

We are also safer when our attention is focused, when we modulate our reactivity and when we can take full responsibility for our behavior—even when we have to work with someone who yells.

We will all make mistakes. In construction, yelling is still common. And last time I checked, almost no one enjoys being yelled at.

It is possible to give fake apologies. They are almost the norm. And a fake apology may be worse than no apology at all. So, if you intend to apologize, do it authentically. Make it stick.

What Constitutes a True Apology?

Sometimes apologies do not work. Sometimes they do. Here are four suggestions you can use to ease the tension in your relationships at work or at home and even achieve a relational breakthrough.

1. Prepare

- Do some personal reflection and find out what you have done or not done that requires an apology. This will require your best emotional intelligence and inner awareness. In the case I described above, it required me to get good coaching from my teacher. It might also involve journaling or full-blown prayer.

- If you get caught up in shame as you prepare (shame = *"I am a mistake"*; on the other hand, remorse or healthy guilt = *"I made a mistake"*), then you might need some extra support to continue.

- Your support should be from someone who is not emotionally involved in the situation. Someone who can be brutally honest with you. If your apology will take the form of a conversation, it will help to practice first with someone.

- If you want a conversation, ask the person involved if you could talk with them about a mistake you made with them. If they say "yes," then continue. If they say "no," do not push. If they will not let you contact them, which can be one of the most challenging situations, you can write them a letter, but be prepared to do some extra inner work to be effective in being authentic (and do not expect a response or a change on their end).

2. Take Action

- Make sure that your tone of voice and body language communicate your sincerity.

- Admit your role in the situation and state it succinctly. The sooner you can get to the point, the better, as they are probably feeling nervous and perhaps are not even fully listening since their flight-fight-freeze response may be activated (thanks to the amygdala in the human brain). Also, if you speak too much, it might recreate the very mistake you have been making: taking up too much airspace!

- Watch for a possible fake apology (see above) and wanting to suggest that they can get over it quickly and move on. You issue the apology; they decide whether to accept it, to wait or to refuse it. This is why you need to come from your heart, as much as you can. It can help you go deeper into why you did what you did, making sure to take full responsibility. *"I said it because I was angry about the situation, but that was a poor way to use my anger."*

- After you tell your story of your role in the situation, it is now important to voice your understanding of how they might feel. *"If someone did that to me, I would feel angry and disrespected."* Or *"I may have this wrong, because I do not know what was going on with you, but I am aware that my saying that may have caused you to feel X, Y or Z."* Or *"My behavior was unacceptable, and I am working to change it."*

3. Listen

- It is now time to truly listen to their response. It's possible that you missed the target of how they are feeling. Genuine listening is a challenge for all of us, especially when we know we screwed up. Yet it is possible.

- The main point is to empathize with them and make eye contact. They might respond with immediate acceptance and love. They might still be angry and worried you will do it again.

4. Consider the Future

- The next step is voicing what you are committed to in the future. For instance, if you forgot the turkey for the company potluck you can say, after your apology, *"I am committed to making sure I bring the turkey next year and will get support to make sure I remember it, and this time it will be an organic one."*

- Finally, and this one may be over the top, but I will throw it out for your consideration. You may want to ask them if they are able to accept your apology or if they need some time. When you do this, you need to ask with as much humility as you can muster. Give them the space and opportunity to say "no." Asking the other person to accept your apology will bring you even more satisfaction, especially if they do accept it. This helps you complete the matter. If they don't accept your apology, it is time to listen again (if they are willing to continue) or to give them time and space to process your regret.

- And then, perhaps the hardest of all: change your behavior. For this part, you might need help.

- Finally, for extra credit, do something positive for them— buy them a gift card to Cabela's, a bag of jerky, tickets to a game, or do some simple act of service.

A fake apology can a bad situation worse. A genuine apology can restore trust and your relationship with a person who is upset with you. Come from your heart and mean it. It will restore your integrity and hold everyone to a higher standard of personal accountability. And if you have higher rank than the other, an authentic apology can be especially powerful. Relationships can mend. Trust can be restored. Create the possibility of a new reality by offering an authentic apology.

CHAPTER THIRTEEN

Courageous Conversations: A Requirement for Safety Accountability

A person's success in life can be measured by the number of uncomfortable conversations he or she is willing to have."

Tim Ferriss, *The Four-Hour Work Week*

Sometimes you need more than an apology. You need a courageous conversation.

Have you heard the one about the monastery where they had just one rule for communication: the monks could only speak two words every ten years? A monk, after his first ten years, went to the abbot and said, *"Bed hard."* The abbot said, *"Bless you, my son. Go in peace."* Another 10 years followed, and the monk spoke his two words again: *"Food awful!"* Again, the abbot replied, *"Bless you, my son. Go in peace."* Ten more years passed, and the monk said, *"I quit!"* And the abbot said, *"Well, it's no surprise to me. You've been doing nothing but complaining for the past thirty years."*

It is extra hard to have a courageous conversation with someone who uses very few words. Many in construction are not very talkative. And when they finally speak, the words can be dramatic: *"You are a jerk." "I quit!" "You're fired!" "I'm done with you!"* These are messages we might hear, or say, after years of unhappiness and "un-had" conversations.

There is another way. We can model the courage to speak up before things get to the quitting or firing point. Catch it earlier. The first time you have that unhappy sensation in your gut, or see someone taking a safety shortcut, find out what is happening and form a plan. If you are triggered, take a little mental break and consider talking to them. Consider bouncing your ideas off a trusted advisor or friend first.

This takes practice, focus and a willingness to break through cultural norms.

Construction workers are not hired because they are experts in courageous conversations. They are experts in building and tearing down things. Some *are* good at having uncomfortable conversations. Many are not. Also, more women are coming into the industry, and in general, they tend to be more skilled communicators. But the average contractor is typically male, physically tough and would prefer not having this kind of conversation, ever.

Courageous conversations are challenging for everyone. Nevertheless, they need to happen if you want to grow your business and create a strong safety culture.

Here are some tips that will help you to prepare yourself for having one of these conversations:

1. Make sure you need to have one. How do you know if it is needed? Look for these signs:

   - The circumstances are stressful, and the stakes are high—perhaps someone's life or limbs are at stake.

   - Emotions are strong—your heart is beating fast and you want to rip their head off.

   - People have different ideas, and they are clashing— you think the answer is A and they think it is B.

If you have even one or two of these, it could be enough for such a conversation. If all three are present, you are risking a lot if you do not initiate a conversation.

2. Check your facts and stories. Make sure you get the information firsthand. If not, then double-check your sources. Everyone tends to make up stories. By this I mean that we all hear or see things, and then we interpret what happened. Just ask any cop to tell you what three different people who saw the same accident said. It is hard to get what Sergeant Joe Friday was always looking for on *Dragnet: "Just the facts, ma'am, just the facts."*

3. Be aware that your own hot buttons may have been pushed, so take a moment to calm yourself by breathing. I recommend the 4-7-8 method taught by Dr. Andrew Weil. See chapter ten. Do this six times and I guarantee you will be calmer.

4. Keep your attitude easy and relaxed.

   It will help you and them if you keep your tone easy and relaxed. There is a tendency, when we have these kinds of conversations, to sound anxious or parental. This is especially true if we have higher rank than the person we are speaking to. So, do your best to approach it as if all is going to end well. Act as if you were sitting down to plan a fishing trip. Take as much emotion out of your voice as possible.

5. Limit the scope.

   By the time you finally get the courage to talk to the other person, often there are multiple problems. Do your best to limit the scope of your conversation. Talk just about one thing. The main issue. You may want to pick the topic that impacts safety or trust the most.

6. Create emotional safety.

    You may think this is over the top. You may think that only physical safety matters. But physical and emotional safety are linked together. If you can't create emotional safety, then physical safety is at risk. Do everything you can to create an emotionally safe situation, including considering where you are meeting, your body language and your tone of voice.

If there is time, sit down and write out what you plan to say. It will help you to follow this "blueprint."

Five-Step Blueprint for a Courageous Conversation

Step One: Purpose. After getting their ok to have the conversation, simply state your purpose in the most positive terms possible. You may be tempted to criticize the other person or bring up the meat of the conversation. *"You have been a total idiot lately!"* or *"Do you have any idea was a dangerous jerk you've been!"* No, those opening statements will not set you up for success. Something more like, *"I value you and want to see you be more effective as a leader..."* Or *"I want to talk to you about some things that will help you in getting along with others."* Or *"I want you to go home to your family alive and well every day, and I have some ideas to help make sure that happens. Can we talk?"*

Step Two: Description of behavior. Make sure to not interpret, judge or make up stories with this part. Keep it to *"just the facts."* Name your observations: just what you could see or hear, like through the lens of a camera. Details matter: *"I noticed you showed up late three out of five days this week."* Or *"I saw that the way you placed the traffic cones on the freeway was not the way you were trained."*

Step Three: Feelings. Share a feeling you have about what is happening. It is possible that sharing of feelings is somewhat uncomfortable or uncommon at your company. That is OK. You can be the one to begin talking about your own feelings: *"I'm frustrated, because I expected..."* or *"I am concerned about you, because of how you are using that piece of equipment."*

Step Four: Consequences. State the tangible consequences the behavior is having on you, others and the job. *"When you arrive late, then X happens." "When you use that equipment in that manner, Y and Z are more likely to happen." "When you do not put the cones out properly on the freeway, we are at serious risk because of..."*

Step Five: Request. Make a clear and simple request of the person you are speaking with: *"So, I am asking you to be on time, or early, every day." "I am asking you to keep a neat jobsite and put tools away where they go, every time." "I am asking you to review the cone safety protocol manual and ask your supervisor to check on your work each day this week."*

If you have never had a conversation with all five steps, do not expect your first one to go perfectly. But each time you have one that goes well, it will get easier to have one more. Make sure to take time to reflect on what went well and what didn't. And then check in with the person, in about a day, to make sure things are ok between the two of you.

If you want to create a culture of safety accountability you will need to have and make sure others are having these kinds of conversations regularly. If you want to be a more effective leader at work and happier in your personal life, you will want to get good at these. The impact of having a positive, courageous conversation can be significant. These will boost the level of trust you have with others, when done well. You will likely need outside support, from time to time, to make sure they go well and end well. It is possible that it will end badly.

When to Not Have That Courageous Conversation

So many people are talking about these conversations. Call them what you will— courageous, crucial, fierce, candid, and constructive. I am all for them. I regularly coach and teach people how to have them, and I have plenty of them myself. But there is also a time to **not** have that uncomfortable conversation.

Here are 12 signs that suggest you should consider **not** having that courageous conversation right. Perhaps it is wiser to wait until a better time, or never have it:

1. **When you feel threatened.** Do you feel angry and ready to fight? Or afraid and ready to run? Are you frozen like a concrete statue? Is your heartbeat accelerated? Is it hard to take a relaxed, deep breath? Do you sense that your lower brain has too much control? Not a great time for a conversation. Take some cool-off time. And do not forget that time in and of itself does not necessarily "heal all wounds."

2. **When the other person's amygdala is activated.** If they are talking faster, seem anxious or upset. If they look dazed or seem to have trouble with words. And remember that some people are very clever at disguising the moments when they are fuming, afraid or feeling threatened.

3. **When you can't see anything from their perspective.** If your thinking is *"I am 100% right and they are 100% wrong; they really need to change!"* you are not in the right frame of mind for a productive conversation.

4. **When you are mad at them.** Calm down first. Six breaths from your diaphragm might be enough. Or you may need three months of counseling. Most likely just a day or two to process things internally or with a trusted friend will help a great deal.

5. **When you are not committed to the relationship.** Whether it is personal or professional, if you have no real investment in the other person, this type of conversation may not go well. If either of you are completely done with the other or with the situation—like ready-to-quit-today done—or if one party can easily walk away, then it might not be a good idea to have this kind of conversation.

6. **When they owe you money or you owe them money and either of you has an emotional charge about that fact.** You might want to settle the money situation first, or ask, *"Can we take the money part off the table for now?"*

7. **When having the conversation is too great of a risk for your business partnership.** If this is the case, it merits some reflection and a conversation with someone else before any decision or process or courageous conversation is considered. Never underestimate the power of a trauma button your message may inadvertently trigger. On the other hand, if there are serious issues you cannot discuss with a business partner, this may be a sign of deeper trouble.

8. **When the other person is highly stressed.** Are they in a low-grade chronic, agitated state? Are they going through one or more of the classic life-stressors? A death in the family, a divorce, a marriage, a new baby, a new house, a serious illness or a Covid-19 trauma? Are they overwhelmed, but are an expert at hiding their inner state? If their face looks blank or slightly frozen, especially around their eyes, it could be a sign they are not fully present.

9. **When you or they are ill, hungry or exhausted.** Make sure you both are well and as calm as possible, since this conversation may create a lot of stress for you both.

10. **When either of you are drinking alcohol or using drugs.** Maybe you do not do either, but so many accidents and injuries happen late at night with the aid of chemicals. Conversational accidents also happen in this state and can become an ugly news story the next day. This is probably not you, but just a friendly reminder for others you may know.

11. **When it's too late at night.** Some people do not sleep well after a courageous conversation. And you are less likely to be on your A-game late in the day. You will need to bring your A-game to this one.

12. **When it's too early in the morning.** Yes, it is possible that you or the other person is not fully awake at 5:15 a.m. Maybe 8:15 a.m. is better.

Only you can tell if the timing is right and if it is best to not have that courageous conversation. Just realize that most people lean strongly toward saying nothing. Then again, there are some very real times when saying nothing is the best decision. So, be honest with yourself as you read through these points and be aware of your relational proclivities.

If you are not sure about whether to have this conversation and need a little help deciding, just reach out to a trusted advisor or trained professional and get it. It is too important, and too difficult, especially when you are triggered, to make this decision totally on your own.

How much did you invest in maintaining your equipment last year? How much are you willing to invest in making sure your people are all maintaining good relationships this year?

CHAPTER FOURTEEN

Improve Your Communication Game: Use the Feedback Loop

"The greatest problem in communication is the illusion that it has been accomplished." —George Bernard Shaw

Y ou will need fewer courageous conversations if you improve the quality of your communication. Take personal responsibility for getting the details right. Just listen to Fr. Vito's story about a situation that happened in the middle of the night.

"Ciao. I'm Fr. Vito, safety chaplain. Are you a-ready to make-a your final confession? If so, then go ahead, forget to confirm those details and ignore those a-safety rules and say all your goodbyes to da family. This could be your last day on the job."
"I have a story about a not-a-so-young married couple with their first child. They were nearly 40 years old and not a-sleeping. Both were exhausted after six months and having a-trouble with da communication. So at 3 a.m. she says to him, "Honey, go downstairs and a-get me the thingamajig on the whatchamacallit." "OK," he says and goes downstairs. He looks all over for that a-thingamajig on a-that whatchamacallit and comes back a-empty handed. What happened? They didn't a-close da feedback loop. It was a communication mistake, but nothing compared to da disaster that could happen when details are lost among your fellow workers working around equipment that could kill them in 5 seconds. Now pray for a miracle. You are going to need one."

Fr. Vito's story is true. I know because I was the one looking for the thingamajig on the whatchamacallit.

What is a feedback loop? In communication, we have several parts: the sender (the quarterback), the receiver (the wide receiver) and the message (the football). In this case, the sender was Kristen, my wife. The receiver was me. The message: *"Get the thingamajig on the whatchamacallit."* There is a fourth part that is often omitted in communication, and especially in construction: the feedback loop. It is also sometimes called "three-way communication." The loop is the message which goes back from receiver to sender, kind of like a boomerang, only instead of clunking you in the head, it clarifies the effectiveness of the communication. The sender knows their message has been received when they get the right feedback.

Communication is complete when both parties understand what is being requested or communicated. I could have asked, *"Which whatchamacallit do you mean? And what thingamajig are you referring to?"* The sender can also initiate the feedback loop. She could have asked, *"Can you tell me what you heard me say?"* and I could have said, with a smile, *"Yes, you said get the thingamajig from the whatchamacallit. Absolute gobbledygook. Please be more specific."*

Because the feedback loop was nonexistent, the result was that nothing was found. It was a simple communication mistake. The root cause: tiredness and a lack of the habit of completing the feedback loop. This kind of thing happens all the time in construction. Every day on hundreds of jobsites supervisors give directions for others to follow. And every day, sometimes because it is loud or maybe there is too much detail or there is interpersonal friction between two workers or because the receiver may not know what a certain word means, the details get lost.

What does it cost you when a large piece of equipment ends up at the wrong jobsite? How expensive is it when supplies are delivered where they are not needed? Mistakes are made and thousands of dollars are wasted every day in construction because details are miscommunicated. And more apropos for this book, people are injured and sometimes killed, partly because communication is incomplete and faulty. The feedback loop rarely happens.

How often does something like this happen at your company? The boss says to the parts runner, *"Hey, Curt get the traffic cones and put them out on the Highway 35 job by end of day, and then get the demo saw to José and ask him to cut that 8-inch pipe into 6-foot segments, and make sure to remind Dave to clean that sewer line with the proper nozzle, and get the skid steer to that other job up north."* What is the typical answer? *"OK, boss. Got it! No problem."*

The new parts runner has no clarity about the details of what he's supposed to do. He gets into his truck, turns to his buddy Joey and says, *"Did you hear all that? How many cones did he want us to put out? Was that 6-foot or 8-foot segments? And did he say what type of pipe that was? Which demo saw, the one with the diamond blade or the one with the abrasive blade on it?"* This is a detail that could lead to a serious injury, if not followed properly. *"And which job up north? There are two. Remind Dave to clean the sewer line with which nozzle? We have six different types of nozzles, which one is the proper one?"* Another detail that can lead to injury. *"And when is end of day? —I'm new here."* Curt is unlikely to call the boss for clarity.

Houston, we have a problem. In fact, we have about six of them in this little scene. Any one of which could lead to lost revenue, major headaches for workers or a serious injury.

In the world of construction, there is a lot of highly detailed information being communicated all the time. Often by men who are not by gender or personality all that detail oriented. And though you might think, this will never change, it is in fact a very solvable problem you have. To solve this problem, you will need to do several things:

1. Admit you have a problem with detailed communication.

2. Commit to changing things, to building a culture where people feel safe enough to change.

3. Train everyone into a new way of communicating. Specifically using the feedback loop every time it is needed

4. Make it habitual—get support and reinforcement to make sure everyone understands and practices the feedback loop.

You can be the one to admit there is a problem. This may take some courage as you may be optimistic and see the world as a glass half full. Maybe you were raised to think, about almost everything, *"No problem."* Or you truly believe that almost nothing is broke, especially things related to communication. Do you often think, *"If it ain't broke don't fix it?"* If so, you are probably very cautious about change.

You can make sure everyone is trained to understand and employ the feedback-loop tool. Good waiters and waitresses do it on every order. It is not that hard. Ideally, the receiver initiates the feedback. *"OK, let's see if I got that, boss."* And they repeat exactly what they heard. Then the sender confirms or fills in gaps. If they get it right, it's a communication touchdown. The sender can also initiate the feedback loop. It doesn't have to always come from the receiver. If the receiver does not ask a confirming question, the sender needs to ask, *"Can you tell me what you heard?"* Just be aware that the sender may get a colorful reply from some, like: *"Yeah, sure, I'll tell you what I heard. I hear you saying that you think I'm stupid!"* This can be avoided by telling them, during the "Feedback Loop Training," that while this answer is clever, it is not the best answer to the question. This tool is not about being smart or stupid. It is about being more detailed and precise in your conversations to prevent inefficiencies and injuries. You want to create a communication culture where the question *"Can you tell me what you heard?"* is a regular and habitual one, and the response is straightforward and detailed, not a snappy, smart-assed one.

During the stress and rush of construction, things get confused and muddy all the time. It helps if the sender is polite and calm about it, realizing that it has nothing to do with intelligence. Good, clear communication is challenging, even in the best of times.

The devil is in the details, right? More accurately, the devil is in the *lack* of details. When you lack details, things can get very bad very fast. This is especially true in construction. I know of a company that had a potentially fatal injury because they did not have clarity on the name of a nozzle and a worker was using the wrong type, with a very high PSI of water pressure running through it. The heavy nozzle came up out of the hole and missed his face by inches and slammed into the side of a steel truck, putting a significant dent in it. Had it hit him squarely in the head, it could have easily killed him at the speed it was traveling. The lack of details in this "near-hit" nearly cost his life.

Great communication takes discipline and precision. To make things even more challenging, it's possible to have a good feedback loop but still have miscommunication. How? Words can be misunderstood. It is said that 500 of the most common English words have over 14,000 meanings (Wallace V. Schmidt et al., "Communicating Globally: Intercultural Communication and International Business," *Sage*, 2007).

In construction, people regularly use different words for the same things. Those who do concrete or underground work use a tool that some call a "demo saw." It has many other names: "chop saw," "cutquick," "Partner saw," "Stihl saw," "German saw," or "maniac saw." It's all the same saw. The question becomes, "Is what you *said* really what they *heard?*" One way to make sure there is no misunderstanding is to use different words for the same idea or detail, and to clarify anything that could be interpreted in more than one way. *"You know, the German saw, the Stihl TS420?"* *"OK, yeah, that quickie saw, the TS420. The one with the blade guard that doesn't have the crack in it?"* *"Yes, that's the saw."* Now you have clarity, in about 7 seconds. The feedback loop will help clarify words that may mean different things to different people. This will save you time and money and, most important of all, prevent injuries.

So, the first thing you need to admit is that sometimes the details are not communicated very well. The second thing is to agree to change that. You need to build a culture where you make it safe for people to regularly say things like *"Let me see if I got that, boss."* And *"Can you tell me what you heard?"* And the third thing is to train everyone to start talking this this. The fourth and final step is to make it habitual and expected that your workers are completing feedback loops every day. All of this will require training and reinforcement. It will not take days or weeks to explain, but it will take outside support and months, of short periods of training, with reinforcement and recognition to embed this new way of communicating into your culture.

Even though confirming details is a small act, it may seem like it takes too much time. But how much time and money are wasted when mistakes are made? How many of your injuries happen, in part, because important details got lost in the rush to get the job done as quickly as possible?

Effective communication travels in a detailed loop, like a boomerang, from the quarterback (sender) to the receiver and back again. Commit to doing this, create a culture where it becomes habitual, and you will have less stress, fewer costly mistakes, lower risk of injury and greater business success. You will score more touchdowns and win the safety accountability game.

CHAPTER FIFTEEN

Giving Verbal Feedback in a Group Setting

There are many kinds of feedback. In the last chapter we learned about "the feedback loop" which is a way to make sure details are clearly communicated between two people. There is another type of feedback, the kind you get or give when things are not going well. Usually, you want to give this type of feedback privately, so as not to humiliate the person you are talking to. And there is a real art to that kind of communication, and we will not be covering that here. But there are times when you need to give feedback to a whole group, which can be incredibly challenging. This was required of me one day and it was a moment of accountability for me.

Thirty-five construction workers gathered for a 90-minute program I was giving in the Midwest several years ago. I could tell they didn't really want to be in the room because a number of them were talking while I was being introduced. And then kept talking as I started presenting.

The topic was "Building a Culture of Safety Accountability." I realized that this situation was going to require my best communication skills judging from the verbal and nonverbal signals I was picking up.

Being from Minnesota, I have lifelong training in being "nice." We tend to be so nice up here in the froze north, that there is a common phrase that others around the country have used to describe us: "Minnesota Nice." This can mean polite, friendly and kind. It can also mean indirect, conflict-avoidant and passive-aggressive. Having spent most of my life in Minnesota, I am impacted by both the good and the bad parts of our culture. Also, though I tend towards being nice, I am not very tolerant of people speaking while someone else is presenting in front of a group.

This shaped a real inner conflict for me, as this group had some chatty fellows. As I began, I noticed what they were doing and gave them each a moderately long stare at various points, attempting to use the laser power of the "evil eye" Miss Olmstead used to give us in eighth grade. My efforts fell far short of Miss Olmstead's.

This was a complex situation because it required breaking a generally agreed-upon communication rule: give praise in public and more critical feedback in private. I would need to break this rule, but not cause undue distraction or make those I was addressing feel disrespected.

About 15 minutes into the presentation, the slide I happened to be on read "Giving Verbal Feedback." I thought, this is perfect timing—they need verbal feedback right now. I also noticed the knot in my stomach. The conflict resolution expert did not want to attempt to resolve this conflict! I did not want to embarrass anyone, and I did not want a fight. Plus, I did not want my intervention to be ineffective. It is possible to make a strong attempt to get people to listen to you and to fail. Failure in this moment could have had serious consequences. This was a crucial moment. Something had to be done to maintain order and to make sure everyone who wanted to learn could do so. Plus, I wanted to maintain my own confidence in my ability to resolve communication challenges.

So, I took a breath, remembered my high rank as the keynote speaker and looked right at the two who were the loudest. I said, *"This slide is about giving verbal feedback. I am about to give some verbal feedback right now."* Wow did that one get their attention. Can't you just see them? They braced themselves for my comments. The power I held in that moment was palpable.

Here is what I said: *"I am a professional. My purpose is to bring you some important information that could make a huge difference for you. It could save a life. And I am noticing that some of you are talking while I'm presenting. I am concerned that others who want to learn here may not have the chance to do so because of you. Maybe you don't want to learn this material. That's fine. I am going to ask you who have been speaking to decide: either stop talking or leave the seminar. It is a sign of disrespect, in most cultures, to speak while another person is speaking."* Their response told me that what I had just done was not the norm. They were not used to someone speaking to them like that.

They clammed up immediately, and no one spoke out of turn again for the next 45 minutes. It was an energizing moment for the whole group. And I also wondered about those two: How were they feeling?

Personal Debrief: How did I do?

- From the standpoint of silencing the talkers, I did well. Two people came up afterwards to thank me for what I did. One of the leaders mentioned my "scolding" the group the next day. So perhaps I could have dropped the line about "disrespect."

- Could I have intervened earlier? Yes. They were talking while their leader was introducing me, and I didn't feel right about that. I chose to ignore that feeling. I could have addressed their behavior right at the beginning. So, by the time I addressed their behavior directly, I was a bit mad at them and couldn't hide it. This is not uncommon for those who are habitually too nice.

- Did I have any curiosity about their points of view and why they were talking? Perhaps I misjudged them as being disrespectful. Was I boring to them? Did they have important input for me or the group? I may never know.

- All in all, I believe my intervention was effective. I got control of the group, and they were then able to hear the information I brought them. I could have gone up to some of them after the event to check in to make sure they understood why I had done that and to see how they were feeling (no doubt some bruised egos).

What are some key ingredients for giving effective verbal feedback in a group setting?

1. Study the situation and discern what you need to say or do.

2. Ground and calm yourself. I did this by taking a few breaths.

3. Be aware of your rank. Your rank is determined by your title, your personality and the type of psychological and personal power you hold. When you have high rank and feel confident giving feedback to anyone, you need to be aware of your tendency to ignore the needs and feelings others have (see chapter eight for more on rank behavior).

4. State your observations in plain language based on observable behavior, with no wiggle room for interpretation: "And I am noticing that some of you are talking while I'm presenting."

5. Make a clear request of them, "either stop talking or leave."

6. Use your rank well. If you have high rank, do not be afraid to fully use it for the good of the group. They are counting on you to lead, to be strong. So be firm, and equally aware of the needs and feelings of others.

7. The general rule is to praise in public and give critical feedback in private. This situation called for me to break

that rule to make sure that everyone had a chance to learn and understand.

8. Check in with them later. This is vital to maintain a positive relationship with them.

May all your verbal feedback be incredibly effective! And when it is not may you dust yourself off and learn from your mistakes.

CHAPTER SIXTEEN

Holding Others Accountable Can Upset the Status Quo

Taking responsibility and holding others accountable for their words and actions can upset the status quo and move you out of your comfort zone. If you are doing it right, it should make you feel a little nervous. I am pretty sure that those two who were talking in that room, during my presentation had some feelings for me that were not warm and fuzzy. And I was also uncomfortable. Acting out of your own integrity and speaking up can cause you and those around you to have emotional reactions. This is true especially if your work culture has a strong norm of avoiding conflict or not speaking up. This is when the real work begins, not when it ends.

This story I am about to tell is based on several situations I've experienced with clients over the years.

Roger was a "rock-star" operator. He could run any machine the company owned, better than anyone else. He held high rank in the eyes of his co-workers, partly because of his skills with machinery and partly because he was a physically large, strong man. Plus, for many years this company had leaders who did not consistently hold others accountable for their actions. This set up a situation ripe for misuse of rank.

Roger had what you might call a long leash. He did not always follow the safety rules. Some he felt were ridiculous.. He also kept his own hours. Some days he clocked in 20 minutes late. Other days he clocked out 30 minutes early. No one seemed to care. The union was not helping with some of these problems.

At some point, the company decided to make changes, which included investing in a process to develop leaders who would hold others accountable. They noticed positive results for the most part, but some workers were especially resistant.

Various leaders attempted to get Roger to comply with the safety rules and clock in and out on time, but with little success. Some of them said, "Just let him be. He has a temper, and yet he gets so much done he's our top producer." So, for a while they let him be. He did seem like a special worker in terms of how productive he could be when he wanted to be.

They then attempted to get him to fall in line with the direction they were going. It was not easy. He raised a stink about it. He began recruiting others to his point of view: that getting the work done was what mattered, not little details like clocking in at exactly the right time or following orders from his supervisors. He made persuasive arguments about why clocking in and out was not in the best interest of work, and how certain safety rules made things more dangerous. He indicated, by his negative comments, that certain leaders were ineffective or not worthy of respect.

Finally, Roger was assigned to Malcolm's crew. Malcolm was a seasoned and respected foreman. He was not interested in coddling Roger one inch—he made that very clear. He and Roger disagreed many times and almost had a physical fight one day. Roger was eventually reassigned to another crew. The foreman on his new crew did not let him get away with anything either. Roger was ultimately fired.

Roger's colleagues had a lot of emotions about the incident. Some felt that Malcolm was too hard on him. Some felt Roger should have been disciplined or fired years earlier. It seemed to really upset the new status quo of culture change. Certain employees said the situation really set back the whole company, which proved that the change process was doomed to fail. They said, *"This has set back this whole sham process."* Others said, *"Look now, all our hard work to change the culture is failing.*" One leader spoke up and said, "No, this is part of the change process. Have you not heard of Bruce Tuckman's model of change? FORM-STORM-NORM-PERFORM. (see Wikipedia, "Tuckman's stages of group development") *"We are now officially in the storm part. We will get through this storm. We are just now beginning the real work of change. This part is necessary."*

No one loves conflict. Not even me and I have a master's degree in it. If they do, we consider them a little crazy. But conflict, chaos and emotional storms are all part of a change process. You cannot have change without the uncomfortable parts. If you are planning to upset the status quo, you can expect that some will *be upset* about your doing that. Prepare to leave your comfort zone.

The key is for leaders to know this and to not panic when it happens. And it will happen, in one form or another.

The best leaders, who are brave enough to engage in a culture change process, will tell their people up front: Expect some trouble to come our way. It is what John Lewis, the politician and civil rights activist, called "good trouble." The key message that leaders need to send is: We can get through it together.

Emotional reactions can be very disturbing to anyone, especially to men who would prefer avoiding them, or are not skilled in dealing with them. When men have strong feelings, there is sometimes a concern that those feelings may lead to physical violence. This needs to be treated seriously. Violence does happen in the workplace. Partly because conflicts have been allowed to escalate too far. Leaders need to intervene earlier and demonstrate how to control their feelings and help others manage theirs. This is the very definition of emotional intelligence. Change processes will upset the way things are usually done, so they require a certain level of emotional intelligence.

And in terms of the threat of physical violence, is it better to let the sleeping dogs lie, or to engage with people who are not following the new expectations and to work with them for a resolution? That is a great question. My belief is that it is better to engage with people who are not following the expectations, if those who are leading have the proper training to do so. How angry do you want that dog to be when he finally wakes up? Be honest, respectful, and direct with your difficult people. Have the conversations you need to have. Let them know what is acceptable and what is unacceptable. Catch them doing things right and praise them whenever you can. Counsel and discipline them when they are breaking or bending the rules. Do not let things escalate. Get your people the training and support they need to deal with the interpersonal challenges right now. This is violence prevention.

We all tend to avoid conflict and trouble. Most of us prefer the status quo, even if it is not perfect. Our brains are hard-wired for survival, and avoiding conflict is part of that survival feature. However, to move through a change process, we need to override that natural tendency to avoid conflict and, instead, move through it with skill. The emotional responses need not thwart us from the goal of transformation.

It is possible. I have seen it happen.

CHAPTER SEVENTEEN

Personal Integrity the Keystone for Trust

"Your mistakes are more visible than you think they are." Mark Breslin

Steve had a lot going on. We had an introductory Thursday morning phone meeting and he had to tend to some urgent matters. He had to get to the airport to fly home and attend to some personal business. It was to be a short but important call for us both. Many guys, at his level in construction, would have blown me off. Not Steve. Although I had never met him in person, and barely knew him, he kept the appointment with me and still got to the airport. That spoke volumes to me about his level of personal integrity.

Integrity is a precondition for accountability. If your people score low on integrity, they will score low on accountability and you will probably not trust them. Neither will others. This can impact both your safety record and your company's profitability.

CEO coach Dr. Fred Kiel lists integrity as one of four *"keystone habits"* in his book *Return on Character*. Kiel defines integrity as *"acting consistently with professed principles, values and beliefs; telling the truth; standing up for what's right; keeping promises"* (*Return on Character*, p. 64). Integrity means following your moral or ethical convictions and doing the right thing in all circumstances, especially when no one is watching you.

Even though you're pretty sure no one will notice this your mistake having integrity means you do the right thing: You fix the mistake. You are true to yourself and would do nothing that demeans or dishonors you or the quality of your work.

Integrity also impacts profitability. Kiel demonstrates powerfully how the character of a C-level leader directly relates to the company's bottom line. He interviewed over 100 CEOs and collected observations from more than 8,000 of their employees. He found that leaders who scored strongly on four keystone habits—integrity, responsibility, forgiveness and compassion—achieved up to five times the return on assets (ROA) than others who scored poorly. Read his book if you want to know more. I know Fred personally, and his research on this book was amazing.

Perhaps you feel you score high on integrity. Or maybe you don't. It is likely that you have some blind spots. Just ask those closest to you to name where your actions and your words have some gaps. I'm pretty sure you will learn a lot. If you have no one close to you who you trust to give you accurate feedback, or if the very idea causes you to feel nervous, maybe your score is not as high as you think.

Mark Breslin, in his potent book *Alpha Dog: Leading, Managing and Motivating in the Construction Industry* states that we all look in the mirror 300-500 times a year. But all we look at is our external, physical selves. We do not look at our internal selves with any regularity. He is right. To Mark's great credit he requires an annual 360 review process for all the workers at his company, and he posts his results on his door each year, for all to view. This is vulnerable, courageous and visionary! I'm not sure I would do it. Would you?

He states that we all have blind spots and are not as well liked as we think we are. This is an unsettling insight, and it rings true for many. It is hard to be a visionary leader with a high level of integrity when our blind spots are keeping us from our true potential.

Breslin observes:

> "Sometimes, once people have gained in confidence or moved up the construction chain of command, they think they no longer

need to examine themselves. This can be a serious mistake, so let me help you see things more clearly.

Those of you already in management positions are not as good leaders as you think you are. Your employees don't like you as much as you think they do. Your team does not admire you like you believe they do. Your mistakes are more visible than you think they are. Your personality is not as winning as you would like. You are not perfect. You are not batting 1.000." (p. 38)

I believe this lack of accurate self-perception Breslin talks about so boldly is partly a function of rank. How so? The root cause of your misperception of your batting average is your high rank. When you are the boss man, people are unlikely to tell you the whole truth about how they experience you and what they think of you to your face, secondly you are not likely to completely hear it even if they did.

People do not like telling the truth to others who outrank them especially if they are part of a culture where telling the full truth about anyone is against the unwritten rules. This is well-documented in politics and in business. It is like fable of the emperor's new clothes. He is made to believe his clothes are beautiful, when in fact he is naked. No one, except the young child, will tell him the truth. If it were the shoemaker who was naked no one would have a problem telling him about his nudity.

This may sound too brash, but I will say it anyway. If you are an alpha male, or an alpha female, you may not feel the need to listen to others. So, even if others were courageous enough to give you some feedback, you could ignore it with relative ease. Your ability to minimize or dismiss their thoughts about you can easily expand to your disinterest in learning about their feelings and needs in general. And before you know it, they doubt that you care for them as people. In addition, you are busy with high level things to tend to. The sabertoothed tigers are at the door. The enemy tribes are closing in. Your high rank, and the responsibilities it brings, can lead to making you less conscious of the needs and feelings of others. This negatively impacts the levels of trust you can build with your leaders. This lack of consciousness, which is common in many companies, is for some, like oxygen deprivation. This is dangerous, even if you are not climbing Mount Everest.

Many times in my life, I have overestimated my level of integrity. It is easy for me to think, *"I used to be a priest, back when priests had instant trust from just about everyone. I am selfless and generous. Integrity is my middle name."* Rubbish. Though I never came close to abusing anyone. Plenty of times, even as a priest, I broke my word, lost my integrity, and did not clean up my people-messes. This work of impeccable integrity is *hard*! As hard as concrete.

Do you know anyone who keeps their word all the time, or nearly all the time? Are they highly respected? Do you know someone who can't seem to keep their word, most of the time? Are they respected or trusted?

On one level, all we really have is our word. Do you do what you say you will do, every time? That would lead to the highest levels of trust possible, right? But no one can do it every time. If you break your word one out of three times, will others develop a high level of trust in you? Probably not. If you break it rarely, they will have more trust in you, and you will get more done.

Every leader I know who wants to build a strong accountability culture is serious about integrity and trust. We now know that trust is a foundation block of any healthy organization and an essential feature of injury prevention for contractors.

David Horsager, a fellow Minnesotan, has built a whole business around the concept of trust. Horsager is teaching people how to create trust in every area of life. He maintains that trust is the most important aspect of business and life and sets a high bar for what it requires to build trust. He writes, *"Trust, not money, is the currency of business and life."* (*The Trust Edge*, Horsager, p. 20) This simple but remarkable book has been widely read and used by businesses all over the world. His challenge is to maintain consistency and to work at building trust with your people every day. Losing trust can be very expensive.

Every contractor I know, especially now, needs to control expenses. Horsager says, *"A lack of trust is your biggest expense."* That is a comment worthy of reflection.

Where do you have a bedrock of trust within your company, and where are you on shifting sand? Where might that shifting sand be exposing you to breaches in safety? And what is the lack of trust and accountability currently costing you?

An friend and owner of a medium-sized company told me that one of his managers was not popular with his direct reports. He said that six workers under that manager had quit in the span of eight months. Clearly there was a lack of good management and a lack of trust. *"What is that costing you, Bill?"* I asked. *"I don't want to think about it, Tom."* *"I am your friend and I care,"* I responded. *"Think about it and let me know if you want help."* He hired me to help him out, and I saved him enough money to buy a few Teslas.

How can you improve trust levels in your work world?

When you have a high-trust culture, you have people who communicate well and can keep their word most of the time. When they do not fulfill on a promise, they apologize sincerely, clean up their mess and act like they mean it. It is not a glib *"Sorry I'm late again guys."* when they show up 20 minutes late for an important meeting. They call ahead or text if they know they will be late. Part of building trust is notifying others beforehand if you can't make the time you agreed to and taking your own breakdown seriously. You do not need perfect behavior to maintain a high level of integrity.

In the construction industry these days there is almost a pandemic of people not keeping their word. Maybe not you and maybe not your company, but I see plenty of people taking the short cut and not maintaining a personal accountability. Have you heard something like this from your sales rep, *"I'll have that rebar order to you by next Tuesday."* On Wednesday you are calling that sales rep because the rebar is not there. On Thursday the general superintendent says, *"Let's meet at 8:30 a.m. tomorrow."* On Friday morning he has three different emergencies before that meeting, caused by delays, weather and mistakes. He cancels the meeting. Maybe he fails to notify the others who are due to be at that meeting. What happens to the trust? What is your word worth? And how do you admit your mistakes? How do you maintain high trust in a world where things change every day? Where deadlines and commitments are often fluid?

You may be thinking, *"Come on Tom, so much is out of my control. This is construction."* David Horsager says, *"There are some circumstances beyond our control, but for the most part, we are the result of our collective actions and decisions."* (The Trust Edge, p. 227)

It is possible to be in communication before the time arrives, to sincerely apologize if you can't keep your word and to recommit to the person and the value of your word. This is one way to maintain your integrity in a world of constant change.

Others will trust you less when you break your word with no warning ahead of time or cleaning up afterward. Plus, your inner self-trust suffers a little each time you break a commitment without checking in with the other.

You can maintain trust by staying in communication about expectations and owning it when the fault is yours. In fact, the best leaders own it even when the fault isn't theirs. *That* is accountability. *"The rebar wasn't there by Tuesday? It is on me; I should have been in closer contact with the salesman."*

Owning mistakes and re-establishing trust is an art. Leaders with a high level of accountability are not afraid to take ownership of what went wrong, including admitting their personal mistakes.

I recommend you read the book *Extreme Ownership* by Jocko Willink and Leif Babin. They were both Navy SEALs, sent to some of the most dangerous battlefields of Iraq about 15 years ago. They not only achieved amazing results during active warfare, but they also returned home and instituted SEAL leadership training that forged a whole generation of SEAL soldiers. One of the more powerful stories is what happened one day in Ramadi when there was a major tactical error and several casualties. (See p. 21-29 of *Extreme Ownership* for all the details.)

As a result of that tactical error compounded by the urban confusion that defined warfare in Ramadi, US soldiers were accidently firing on their own people: "friendly fire." One man was killed (he was an Iraqi fighting with US troops) and a Navy SEAL took some shrapnel to the face, other Iraqis who were with us were injured. The situation was terrible. Getting killed in battle is horrible enough. Killing one of your comrades is even worse.

A whole team of military investigators arrived on scene soon after the incident, the investigating officer, the commanding officer, the command master chief and the senior enlisted SEAL. They asked Jocko to prepare a brief. He knew that meant they were looking for someone to blame. He studied every angle of the grave mistake to find the proper place to put the blame. He identified multiple things that happened to create confusion, and various units, leaders and soldiers who had not done their job perfectly. He thought he uncovered all the root causes. But there was something missing. There was a piece he could not identify. Then he realized that there was only one person to blame: him. He had not been with the sniper team at the right time. He had not help to control the rogue element of Iraqis who entered the compound. He was responsible for the whole mission.

He bravely stood up before the investigating team as well as the soldiers who were there. He asked his teammates, *"Whose fault was this?"* Several of his teammates spoke up to courageously take the blame. Jocko kept saying *"No, it wasn't your fault?"* Finally, he said *"Negative. You are not to blame. . .there is only one person to blame for this: me."*

He knew that this kind of ownership could have easily gotten him fired. Instead, it earned him greater respect than ever. And he reports that this kind of ownership, in the end, saved lives because it allowed him to humbly re-establish his authority, deeply examine everything that went wrong and learn from the deadly error.

When people communicate well, admit mistakes and take this extreme level of ownership, you have a safer battlefield and a more-protected workplace. You also will have greater interpersonal awareness, a higher level of trust and better relationships.

"You really want me to admit my mistakes? Shouldn't I hide my mistakes and faults, so no one sees them?" No. You want to be transparent. If you are hiding mistakes, you are likely in a low-trust culture. Be authentic and open. Do you really think others don't see your faults?

You don't need to publicly admit every single little error, like the time you left the mustard out on the breakroom counter all day. But people know if you tend to be sloppy, or maybe too aggressive, or perhaps inclined to micromanage others. They see your way of being. They know that you have just taken your fifth text during your 20-minute meeting with them. You can't hide stuff like that. If your way of being, or your specific behavior, leads to a mistake or an irritation that impacts others at work, then just take responsibility for your behavior and sincerely recommit to who you want to become. You are what you do.

If you should have had a conversation with someone and you did not, and it leads to an unhappy co-worker or a risky situation, then take ownership for that conversation you did not have.

Your lawyer may not advise this. Some attorneys would say, *"Let me handle this. Do not go telling people what you didn't do, or what you did do that led to a situation. It could get you into legal trouble."* But this is one of the problems with our legally oriented culture and with the integrity level of leaders in our organizations: We want to hide our mistakes, partly out of embarrassment and partly from fear of legal trouble or financial loss.

I believe that in the long run, you will have more financial losses if you attempt to cover up your mistakes. What happens in Vegas doesn't stay in Vegas. Not anymore. It never really did. The word will get out. Plus, you will lose trust in yourself. So, why not tell on yourself? That way you have a chance of restoring and maintaining your integrity, and you get to have more control over the story.

If you oversee training of new workers, and one of them strained their back because they did not lift a manhole cover properly because you felt there was not enough time to teach proper lifting of manhole covers or you were too disorganized, then you are part of the root cause. You know it, they know it and anyone else they have told knows it. If you hide your part, they will know it and resent you for it. It will lead to a reduction in your integrity.

So just admit your mistake, without any excuses, and accept the consequences. If you work for a company where you need to hide all your mistakes, how happy are you about being there?

If an older worker, who was working on a two-man crew with a hard-working person 15 years his junior, came to you and complained of back pain, what would you do? I know a leader who decided to ignore that complaint. That older worker threw his back out a few weeks later. Who ultimately takes the ownership for that? And what type of leader would own and attempt to repair this mistake?

You will stand out as a person of unusual integrity if you repair your mistakes, even if it costs you. *Especially* if it costs you. You will shine like a beacon because few people live like this. You can say, *"I did not show him the proper way to lift manhole covers, and I am at fault."* Not *"I was too busy to teach him every way of lifting."* Not *"I can't quite recall what I said."* Not *"I wasn't the only one who could have taught him the right way."*

Take full responsibility and acknowledge the impact your mistake may have had on others. Could you suffer legal or workplace consequences? Yes, you could. I say man up, woman up, and admit your mistake. Admit it with the person who was impacted, and with others who know the situation. And who knows the situation? Perhaps many people.

The White House Office of Consumer Affairs found that a dissatisfied customer tells 9-15 people about their poor experience, and nearly 13% of those dissatisfied customers tell more than 20 people. A dissatisfied customer is no different from a dissatisfied employee: They tell more people than you may know, and they will rarely talk to you about it.

My mom used to apologize when she made a parenting mistake, like yelling too loudly at us or forgetting something that was important to us. She owned it, without shame and without excuses. That was a great example for me, and one that has made it relatively easy for me to admit my mistakes now, when I see them, both at home and at work. The hard part for me, at times, is seeing them.

Maybe your family modeled taking responsibility for mistakes; maybe they modeled hiding them. Or maybe they did some of both. Whatever your background, you can begin to take full responsibility today, and regain the integrity you have lost attempting to hide your mistakes.

When you give your word and break it without any comment or explanation, that can destroy trust. Over time, people no longer believe you will do what you say. Your word has no integrity. You will eventually lose respect.

So, be careful when you give your word. Consider whether you can truly get that task done in the time that it will require to be done in excellence. And get some details on how they want it done, by when. Make sure you understand the results they want. Practice the feedback loop before finalizing your word.

You are a leader. They are watching you and keeping score. You may think you know the score, but the odds are good you do not. Doing a 360 process is one way to get honest feedback. Just make sure the process is set up well and facilitated with the utmost professionalism, since these things can go awry.

If you are habitually late, with no apology or explanation, you have lost your time-integrity. You can't expect others around you to be on time either. According to Les Hill, owner of Les Is More Coaching, *If you lose integrity in one area, it impacts them all.* Can you be habitually late and have perfect integrity in every other arena of your life? Highly unlikely.

And conversely, if we reclaim integrity in one area, it positively impacts the other areas. You will grow your integrity and the level of trust others have in you. You will also raise the bar of accountability for all in your circle of influence as you take responsibility for your whole life. Doing this will likely require the support of an outside professional. Someone like a coach or communication consultant.

Your level of personal integrity shapes the quality of relationships you have with co-workers. And the nature of your co-worker relationships impacts the level of safety accountability in your organization.

We all tend to be out of integrity from time to time in at least one area of our lives. Where is there a gap in your integrity today? Not sure? Just ask anyone who knows you and is honest. Then repair the breach. Your mistakes and missing integrity are more visible, and more costly, than you think they are.

Your personal integrity is one of the keystones to your whole program of safety accountability. It is the main stone that holds the whole structure together. Make it a central priority and you will grow both your business and your capacity to influence others.

CHAPTER EIGHTEEN

The Impact of the Man Box Culture

I want to share some of my experiences living and working in male-dominated culture. For more than ten years I lived among men in the seminary, at the University of Notre Dame, in South Bend, Indiana, in Kenya, and a variety of other locations in the States during the 80s and 90s. It was a good life. I enjoyed the education, the fine teachers and priests who had a huge positive influence on me, being a minister, and more than a few exciting Notre Dame footballs games.

In 1986 I was living in Colorado with a bunch of seminarians. We were spending a year of our lives living in the mountains like monks and discerning whether to take vows for a lifetime as Caholic priests. We resided in a gorgeous, marbled mansion in the Rocky Mountains at the foot of Pikes Peak. The three vows were "poverty, celibacy and obedience." We used to say, "*Wow, if this is poverty, bring on celibacy!*"

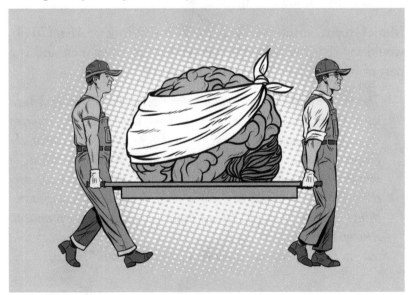

We were in the basement of the mansion one night having a few beers and playing guitars. At one point I needed to get something upstairs. We had only been there a few weeks and I was not yet used to the low ceilings, especially in the stairwells. I bounded up the stairs and hit my head hard on a low marble ceiling. I was briefly knocked out. The first thing I thought when I came to was *"I'm OK"* and then, *"Wow, does my head hurt!"* The guys could tell I was *not* OK, but I assured them I was. And I certainly didn't say anything about my feelings. They knew I probably had a concussion, so they insisted that they would wake me up several times during the night to check on me, which they did. I kept insisting I was fine. I survived it despite my stubborn hard headedness, or in this case, maybe because of the hardness of my head.

I learned this way of being, ignoring physical pain and not talking about feelings, growing up in a Roman Catholic family with lots of brothers and a father steeped in military discipline. He could be critical of those who expressed emotion and I got the message. This "I'm-OK-when-I'm-knocked-down" idea is kind of funny from one point of view, but tragic and potentially dangerous from another. It is a particular way of being that is especially well known to men.

Mark Greene, author of *The Little #MeToo Book for Men* (2018), would say that my behavior was typical for many men and is a part of what he calls "the man box culture." He writes:

> *The man box refers to the brutal enforcement of a narrowly defined set of traditional rules for being a man. These rules are enforced through shaming and bullying, as well as promises of rewards, the purpose of which is to force conformity to our dominant culture of masculinity. Go to any middle school...in America. Ask the boys there to tell you the rules for being a man. They'll all tell you the same things. Always be tough. Always be successful. Always be confident. Always have the last word. . . . But one of the first rules they will tell you is that "real men don't show their emotions." (p. 16)*

Therefore, it makes sense to ask men in construction (and of course women, too, in the rare instances when we work with them) how they are feeling and not let them just say, *"Fine."* Most do not like this at first, but then they appear to appreciate it later. Men have a lot of feelings. They just don't always know what they are or how to voice them. And I firmly believe they will be happier and safer as they begin to grow their emotional awareness.

Why are they safer? When men (and women) can name and express their own feelings in a trusted environment, they are physically and emotionally in a less risky position. They may be less tempted to pick up that 150 lb. manhole cover by themselves and more likely to be aware of their own well-being. Once they are more aware of their own well-being it is a short jump to proactively look out for the safety of others. Plus, awareness and proper expression of one's own feeling-state reduces stress and can prevent workplace violence.

Showing empathy after an injury of a co-worker, even a minor injury, can help you to break out of the man box voice that says, "Suck it up buddy like I would!"

Construction companies with personnel who understand the dangers of the "man box culture" are doing several new things.

They are starting to talk about well-being and offering stress-reduction resources to workers. They are including the idea that emotions matter, even to guys working in construction where feelings often take a back seat to the daily physical grind.

Some companies are using one of the assessment tools developed by the military years ago. It is known as an after-action report, or AAR. AARs are quick, structured debriefing reports held after a military operation to review what happened, discover what went well and what didn't and learn as much as possible about why.

I first learned about the AAR from a friend named Dr. Jim Lynn. Jim is a veteran of the Vietnam War and has deep respect for military values and culture. He also has a long history of helping individuals and organizations make productive behavioral changes. He has taught me a lot about the way those in the military process their learning after a military action. There are three steps to the basic AAR, originally developed by the US Army:

1. What happened?

2. Why did it happen?

3. How could it be done better next time?

   Dr. Lynn explains that the Marines, one of the toughest branches of the US military, add a fourth component. He always asks the groups he works with if they know what the Marines add. They almost never know. I did not know either, so I called up an old business friend, Brian Delahaut. He is a Marine and an owner of MK Diamond based in California. Brian explains that the Marines do add a fourth question:

4. How did this situation/action affect you? (which Dr. Lynn phrases as "How did it make you feel?")

Why should the super tough, incredibly well-trained and "semper fidelis" (always faithful) Marines add this fourth step to their AAR? Perhaps they understand the value of emotional intelligence. Why should it matter how someone feels during and after military action? Because the Marines know that the way we feel impacts the way we act. Some have more control over the natural fight/flight/freeze response, and some have less control. Knowing how someone was feeling can help everyone understand what happened and how to do it better or avoid it completely next time.

The Marine-style AAR model is perfect for any significant incident in construction, especially where there has been a serious injury or a significant near-hit. It could be used to determine root causes and to prevent future injuries, especially if the person trusts others enough to share how they felt during the situation.

I know it's not common for those in male-oriented cultures like the military and construction to talk about feelings. But if the Marines can do it, why not construction workers?

Almost every meeting I start begins with a brief check-in. This includes everyone naming a current emotion they are experiencing. And "good," "fine" and "OK" do not count. Requiring people to identify their own feelings is the beginning of a new level of emotional intelligence, and a key competency of effective leaders.

A complete shut-down of emotions is one of the reasons men suffer from depression. And untreated depression + the physical pain that comes from decades of physical labor + the social isolation that can happen because of extended travel + the broken marriages and relationships that often affect people + addiction to chemicals or alcohol + an economic downturn across society sets up a situation where men in construction are extra vulnerable to suicide. According to Cal Beyer, with CSDZ, a Holmes-Murphy company, and an industry expert on suicide, more construction workers are believed to die by suicide than all occupational deaths combined. According to the Construction Industry Alliance for Suicide Prevention, the CDC reports that construction occupations have "the highest rates of suicide" across all other industries. (see https://preventconstructionsuicide.com/)

So, to ensure worker well-being, including reducing the risk of suicide, a part of your safety accountability program needs to be emotional intelligence education. There are many ways to improve the emotional intelligence of workers in construction. One of the main ways is described in *The Emotional Intelligence Quick Book*, by Travis Bradberry and Jean Greaves. It is a quick, easy read with some real gems. Bradberry and Greaves teach that you can improve your emotional intelligence by doing certain practices that develop the pathway between your limbic system and your prefrontal cortex. *"The more you think about what you are feeling and do something productive with that feeling—the more developed this pathway becomes."* (*The Emotional Intelligence Quick Book*, p. 13). This is a simple but profound insight. Here are some ideas for you to grow your emotional intelligence:

- If you are angry—name the feeling, share it with someone and get some physical exercise: go for a walk or a run.

- If you are sad—name the feeling, share it with someone and watch a sad movie.

- If you are frustrated—name the feeling, share it with someone and change expectations. Or change the situation that led to your frustration.

- If you are feeling anxious—name the feeling, share it with someone and appreciate someone. Gratitude and anxiety can't survive together in the same house.

One of the truly successful consultants and trainers in this area is Brent Darnell. (His company is also the publisher of this book.) Brent has logged hundreds of hours training people from the Architectural, Engineering and Construction (AEC) industry. They have benefited from his expertise on emotional intelligence. He and his wife have taught meditation and yoga to contractors! They see these disciplines as important for the mental and physical well-being of workers. And for higher levels of excellence. Brent writes, *"All things being equal, the people who excel are the ones with higher levels of emotional intelligence."* (Brent Darnell, *The People-Profit Connection*, p. 26.) If you like what this chapter is about, I recommend that you look at Brent's book.

Not only emotions, but sometimes, in tough-guy cultures other basics like diet, sleep and exercise are devalued.

How many events have I attended at construction companies, where the food served is doughnuts, pizza or grilled meat? How about a salad? Or maybe a vegetable. The food you eat is the fuel for your body's engine. It matters what you put in.

Darnell says that when he's coaching a worker known for being a little rough around the edges one of the first things he asks about is diet. "What did you have for breakfast?" The reply is often, "A cup a coffee." "And then what?" "Maybe a Red Bull or a doughnut." And by 11:15 a.m. this guy is yelling at people. Could it be related to diet? Absolutely. Is it only diet? Probably not. He may have other issues such as a back problem, some situational depression and/or an inflated sense of ego. Plus, there just might be many things going wrong on the construction project.

My wife, Kristen Wernecke, wrote a book called *Choosing Conscious Health for a Vibrant Life*. For over thirty years she has practiced as massage therapist, healer and a wellness specialist. She really understands how diet impacts well-being and productivity. In chapter five of her book, she recommends the following ideas for a healthy diet. Eat protein from vegetables (like beans) as well as organic, grass fed or free-range livestock as much as possible. If you eat meat not labeled in this way you ingest hormones in these animals which will over time have a negative effect on your body. Eat whole grains such as rice, oats, quinoa, millet, barely and whole grain bread. Lower your consumption of foods with hydrogenated (trans) fats, as well as foods high in cholesterol and dairy. Reduce your intake of processed sugar, caffeine, energy drinks and corn syrup. In the year 2,009 more than 50% of Americans consumed one half pound of refined sugar a day, which is 180 pounds per year! In the year 1800 the average consumption was 4 pounds per year. Try raisins, dates, nuts, and fresh fruits instead. The more organic the better. If you doubt the value of good eating just look at the diet of any world class athlete. They are careful and intentional about what they feed their "machine." If this all of this is too much for you, you can start out your health food journey with the Impossible Whopper.

Exercise might not seem important to people who work outside, lifting heavy things and physically moving all day long. Remember, stretching is exercise, and if you are doing heavy labor, you need to be stretching those muscles or you will sooner or later run into trouble. Even if you are the Walter Payton of construction. Also, you may be in great muscular shape but what will keep you alive is cardiovascular health, which comes from vigorous exercise, where your heartrate is elevated for about twenty minutes.

We all know that sleep is vital to maintain optimal health. We rebuild our cells and refresh our minds during sleep. When we lack sufficient rest, we are tired and more prone to lapses in attention, which is a potential safety hazard. I know I sound like your mother when I ask, are you doing all to make sure you are getting proper rest? Exercise, meditation, and proper diet is helpful for developing good sleep habits.

The unwritten rules of man box culture are deeply engrained. The rules for staying part of the club will not easily go away. Yet they can be balanced with sensible, scientifically proven methods that improve worker well-being.

I am hearing more and more construction workers talking about diet and other aspects of well-being. A company recently hired me to give a workshop and a keynote on well-being at their annual safety meeting. When safety and well-being are used in the same sentence, I know that the leaders truly care for their people and are offering resources to improve the lives of employees.

Safety accountability and well-being resources must include emotional and relational awareness. Our ability to relate and communicate is directly related to safety. When we introduce practices that contribute to worker well-being, we become advocates for a healthier way of being and safer jobsites. And we are freeing men from a dangerous box.

CONCLUSION

I am guessing that you are the change agent in your company. That is why you are reading this book and others are not. You are the one who is considering this important work. Maybe you have done some leadership development, and you have attempted some communication improvement, but not much happened and you feel that something substantial is missing.

You may have moved around the deck chairs, but the ship is going the exact same direction.

Yes, there are risks in embarking on this kind of change in a tough guy culture like construction. You will be criticized. Some will openly oppose your ideas. Even though all you are doing is directed at the safety and well-being of others, some will still resist your efforts. They may even recruit others to join in resisting you. You will be dumbfounded.

Don't be surprised. This work of culture change can be threatening to some and might even made you a bit nervous. I have a master's degree in conflict resolution and have spent hundreds of hours attempting to facilitate non-violent resolution to conflict, and I still get nervous doing this work. Just the idea of change is an emotional trigger for some that sets off their fight or flight response. Be ready for that. Be prepared for a good battle on some days. Do your best to put your ego on the shelf. You may need to ask for help.

On the other hand, you don't have to do any of this. You can stay on the path you are on now. You can wait for another time to embark on this kind of work. You do not have to rise up and lead a revolution and you do not have to chop anything down. You can maintain the level of teamwork and communication you currently have. You can decide it is ok that your people do not speak up when speaking up is needed—even though you know it increases the risk of injury. You can hope and pray that their silence does not contribute to a serious injury or worse. No one has to have a courageous conversation. No one has to take the kind of extreme ownership Jocko Willink, the Navy SEAL took when he said about the friendly fire casualties that happened on his watch, "There is only one person to blame for this: me."

The decision is yours. Rise up now and begin the bold revolutionary work, or wait for another time, or maintain the status quo.

Should you choose to do this kind of powerful work, It would be my honor to partner with you or lead you to someone else who can.

Finally, I leave you with the inspiring words, penned by Margaret Fuller, 19th century American journalist, translator, and women's rights advocate,

"May God keep you safe until the word of your life can be fully spoken."

APPENDIX

The Top 10 Problems with Safety Directors

I have met and been in communication with hundreds of safety directors over the past 20 years. They have extremely challenging jobs. Many are working hard, enjoying their work and making a real difference. Super accountable leaders. And just as many do not show signs of being motivated and do not appear to be as effective as they could be. Some of the reasons are beyond their individual efforts, and some of the reasons lie squarely on their shoulders. Here are the top 10 problems as I have seen them and some suggested solutions. Not all safety professionals experience these or are defined by them, though many do and are.

Top 10 Problems

1. They are not properly supported by owners and top managers. They have an insufficient level of power to influence.

2. They wear too many hats (especially in smaller companies).

3. They are overwhelmed by the ever-expanding list of rules and requirements.

4. They are burned out. They just don't care that much anymore.

5. They get into "safety policing." They are too focused on catching people doing it the wrong way, either because

of the culture of their company or because of their own personality (or both).

6. Their work feels boring. Much of safety can be boring without regular bursts of creativity.

7. They do not have a big enough vision. They settle for the minimum.

8. They lack the interpersonal skills and "power skills" to build trusting relationships. They are not able to coach, affirm and support those doing the physical work.

9. They lack the full integrity required to build high levels of trust. They do not do at home what they preach about at work.

10. They do not stay in their role for enough years to make a real difference in shaping culture.

Top 10 Solutions

1. Get the safety director the proper support they deserve and need to be effective. Many company leaders say, "Safety is #1," with words, but their actions say, "The Almighty Dollar is #1." Make sure that top C-level leaders spend time with them regularly, verbalize appreciation for the work, and offer them competitive salaries.

2. Take some hats off them. I understand that very small companies will need workers who can fill several roles. But if your company is big enough and sufficiently profitable, find a way to let them focus on safety full time. It is likely you are underestimating the time and interpersonal skills it takes to be truly effective at building a strong safety culture.

3. Help to locate the specific sources of overwhelm and support them to proactively manage their own stress levels.

4. Know the signs of burnout. Show them how to move through burnout and reengage in their work.

5. Make sure they are not overly critical of others. Help them catch people doing things properly and focusing on the positive. Get them some formal co-worker feedback, with the support of an outside professional.

6. Help them find ways to engage in the work of safety accountability and feel excited about their role. Make sure they have chances to network with other safety professionals.

7. Help them with vision by getting them some quality coaching or other support.

8. Give them resources to develop their communication and leadership skills. Good safety leadership requires excellent people skills as well as technical expertise. They need to have the ability to influence, motivate and inspire others. They must have the capacity to build trusting relationships, handle resistance, and occasionally resolve conflict. They also have to be able to track and understand technical details. And do not forget the importance of their "power skills." Do they fully understand how rank functions and how to best use the power they do have? All should have a basic level of courageous conversation training.

9. Support them in having impeccable integrity: actions and words that consistently match. Have them work with an integrity coach (I would highly recommend Les Hill, of www.LesIsMoreCoaching.com or myself).

10. I know of companies that treat the safety director role as a revolving door. Make sure you hire the right person and

help them to stay in that role for at least five years. Many organizational development professionals find that true culture change in most companies takes three to five years of focused efforts. In construction it can take even longer. To reap the benefits of your investment make sure they have all they need to do their job successfully. The lives of your workers and the growth of your business depend on it.

CPSIA information can be obtained
at www.ICGtesting.com
Printed in the USA
FSHW020059030421
80066FS